THE UK NINJA® Foodi SMARTLID

Delicious Traditional British Recipes with Pictures using European measurements

KEEP WARM

AIR FRY

START STOP

Introduction

This large-capacity smart multi-cooker that can do everything

It's a pressure cooker, oven, hob and air fryer; the Ninja Foodi Smartlid™ allows you to prepare recipes that you usually find difficult to prepare with standard cooking equipment. So, if you're craving chicken pot pie or sweet bread pudding, the Ninja Foodi can get it done for you!

In this recipe book you`ll learn how to use your Ninja Foodi Smartlid like a pro with step by step guide & easy-to-follow instructions to make a delicious traditional British recipes.

LAUGHTER IS BRIGHTEST WHERE FOOD IS BEST

——

Desserts

Breakfast & Sides

Beef

Poultry & Seafood

Vegetables

HOW TO USE NINJA FOODI SMARTLID

The Basics

In this section we are going to show you how to get started with your Ninja Foodi Smartlid™, do a brief overview of the cooking functions and provide a few tips. So, let's get started on how to use the Ninja Foodi Smartlid™ !

"NINJA FOODI SMARTLID™ DOES IT ALL. YOU CAN REPLACE YOUR AIR FRYER, PRESSURE COOKER, SLOW COOKER FRYING PANS AND EVEN YOUR OVEN."

It's a pressure cooker, oven, hob and air fryer; the Ninja Foodi Smartlid™ allows you to prepare recipes that you usually find difficult to prepare with standard cooking equipment. So, if you're craving chicken pot pie or sweet bread pudding, the Ninja Foodi can get it done for you!

WHAT IS THE NINJA FOODI SMARTLID MULTI-COOKER?

This next-generation multi-cooker provides more exciting ways to prepare your favourite meals, including the innovative Combi-Steam Mode. It combines steam and convection to produce juicy, quick, and crispy results! Steam will foster moisture and flavour into your food as it cooks by using the liquid added to the pot with your recipe ingredients. The end result? Food that is tender and moist on the inside and crisp on the outside.

Only one lid is required for ALL functions! As a result, there is no longer need to store the pressure cooking lid while using air fryer lid.

The SmartLid has a unique way of keeping the lid closed.Instead of screwing on the pressure cooking lid, simply lower it into position and slide the slider to the desired cooking function.

HOW TO USE THE NINJA FOODI SMARTLID MULTI-COOKER?

1.Pressure Mode:

- Open the lid, Insert the cooking pot.

Always use lift tab to open & close lid to keep your hand away from hot steam and heat.

- If recipe requires browning meat/chicken or Sautéing onion, just move the SmartSlider to AIR FRY/HOB. Select SEAR/SAUTÉ and adjust the temperature. Select START/STOP, add oil. <u>If the recipe do-not require browning/Sautéing skip this step.</u>

- Add Ingredients.
- Close the SmartLid.
- Move the SmartSlider to Pressure.

- Using arrow buttons, set time and High or Low pressure for the recipe.

- When cooking is complete and the steam is released, move SmartSlider to the AIR FRY/HOB position, then open lid.

2. Combi-Steam Mode:

- Open the lid, Insert the cooking pot.
- Add the required liquid specified by the recipe.
- Add Ingredients on the Deluxe Reversible Rack or Cook & Crisp Basket (as it will specified by the recipe).

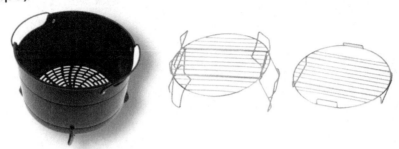

- Close the SmartLid.
- Move the SmartSlider to COMBI-STEAM. Once you've chosen a mode, use the dial to choose your desired function.

You can choose between :

1. STEAM MEALS
2. STEAM AIR FRY
3. STEAM ROAST
4. STEAM BAKE
5. STEAM BREAD

- Using arrow buttons, set time and temperature for the recipe.

- When cooking is complete, open lid.

3. Air Fry/ Hob Mode:

- Open the lid.
- Add Ingredients on the Deluxe Reversible Rack or Cook & Crisp Basket (as it will specified by the recipe).

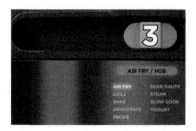

- Close the SmartLid.
- Move the SmartSlider to Air Fry/ Hob. Once you've chosen a mode, use the dial to choose your desired function.

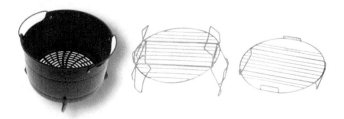

You can choose between :

AIR FRY, GRILL, BAKE, DEHYDRATE, PROVE, SEAR/SAUTÉ, STEAM, SLOW COOK, YOGURT, KEEP WARM.

- Using arrow buttons, set time and temperature for the recipe.

- When cooking is complete, open lid.

BAKEWELL TART

 1 Hour   Serves 12

Ingredients:

Pie Crust:
- 200g plain flour
- 2 tbsp icing sugar
- 125g cold butter, grated
- 1 egg yolk
- 2 tbsp water

Filling:
- 180g softened butter
- 180g caster sugar
- 3 eggs
- 180g ground almonds
- 1 tsp almond essence
- 200g raspberry conserve
- 25g flaked almonds

Steps:

1. In a bowl, add flour, butter, egg yolk and sugar. Mix until mixture resembles large crumbs. Gradually drizzle in water, until mixture starts to form a ball and holds together. Don't over mix.
2. Transfer dough onto lightly floured surface. Flatten into a circle, transfer into a 23-cm pie tin. Press down and trim edges. Top with baking paper, Fill with dried beans. Place tin on Ninja Foodi middle rack.
3. Close lid and move the slider to AIR FRY/HOB. Select AIR FRY and set temperature to 160° C/320° F. Set time for 15 minutes. Press START/STOP to begin cooking.
4. In a large bowl, add all filling ingredients (except conserve) and whisk until combined and smooth. Spread conserve over pastry base. Pour filling into pie crust, then sprinkle with flaked almonds. Place tin back on the Ninja middle rack.
5. Close lid and move the slider to AIR FRY/HOB. Select AIR FRY and set temperature to 160° C/320° F. Set time for 35-40 minutes until golden brown. Press START/STOP to begin cooking.
6. Remove from Ninja Foodi and let cool completely. Place in the refrigerator to fully set. Serve.

SPOTTED DICK

30 Minutes   Serves 8

Ingredients:

- 250g self raising flour
- Pinch of salt
- 125g shredded suet
- 180g mix fruit
- 80g caster sugar
- 1 lemon zest
- 1 small orange zest
- 150ml milk

Steps:

1. In a large bowl, add all ingredients and mix until combined. add more milk if needed.
2. Transfer in a pudding dish, cover with foil.
3. Add 240ml water to bottom of Ninja Foodi. Place bottom layer of Deluxe Reversible Rack in the lower position. Place the pudding dis on top of rack, then place rack in the pot.
4. Close lid with valve is in seal position, move slider to pressure, select STEAM and set to 12 mins.
5. When cooking is complete. Move slider to Air Fry/HOB to unlock the lid, then carefully open it. Remove apples to serving plates. Serve warm.

GOLDEN SYRUP STICKY DATE PUDDING

🕐 40 Minutes   👤 Serves 6

Ingredients:

- 4 tbsp golden syrup/date syrup
- 60g butter
- 60g light brown sugar
- 110g apple sauce
- 100g self-raising flour sifted
- 1 tsp baking powder
- 100g dried dates, sliced, pitted & chopped
- 1 tsp cinnamon powder
- 2 tbsp milk

Steps:

1. Grease 4 180ml/4oz. ramekins with butter/cooking spray.
2. In a mixing bowl, add butter and sugar, mix using a hand mixer until combined. Add apple sauce, flour, baking powder and cinnamon. mix with spoon until combined. Add dates and milk. mix with spoon until combined.
3. Divide batter evenly between prepared ramekins. Cover with foil.
4. Add 250ml water to bottom of Ninja Foodi. Place bottom layer of Deluxe Reversible Rack in the lower position. Place the ramekins on top of rack, then place rack in the ninja pot.
5. Close the lid with valve is in the seal position and move the slider to COMBI-STEAM. Select Steam & Bake set temperature to 170°C/340°F, and time to 35 minutes. Select Start/Stop to begin cooking.
6. When cooking time is complete, use a skewer to check the pudding. If it comes out clean, the pudding is ready. If not, bake for a further 5-10 minutes covering with foil. Then carefully remove and let cook slightly then serve.

BARA BRITH

🕐 1 Hour   👤 Serves 5

Ingredients:

- 375g dried mixed fruit soaked overnight in 300ml hot tea and 100g Dark Brown Sugar
- 1 tsp Mixed Spice
- 250g Self raising Flour
- 1 egg, whisked

Steps:

1. Add flour, mixed spices and egg into the bowl of soaked mixed fruit. Mix until all combined.
2. Line a 23x13cm loaf tin with baking paper. Pour the batter into lined loaf tin.
3. Add 360ml water to bottom of Ninja Foodi. Place bottom layer of Deluxe Reversible Rack in the lower position. Place the tin on top of rack, then place rack in the pot.
4. Close the lid with valve is in the seal position and move the slider to COMBI-STEAM. Select Steam & Bake set temperature to 180°C/356°F, and time to 1 Hour. Select Start/Stop to begin cooking.
5. When cooking is complete, Move slider to Air Fry/HOB to unlock the lid, then carefully open it. use a skewer to check the bread. If it comes out clean, the bread is ready. If not, bake for a further 5-10 minutes covering with foil.
6. Let cool then slice and serve with tea.

PUMPKIN SPICE BAKED APPLES

🕐 30 Minutes   👤 Serves 4

Ingredients:

- 4 medium apples, top removed & cored
- 113.5 g unsalted butter (softened)
- 1 tsp vanilla essence
- ½ tsp nutmeg
- 1 tbsp cinnamon
- 4 tbsp brown sugar
- 60g walnuts (chopped)
- 60g raisins

Steps:

1. In a mixing bowl, add brown sugar, butter, walnuts, raisins and pumpkin spice. Stir to combine.
2. Spoon mixture into each apple.
3. Add 240ml water to bottom of Ninja Foodi. Place bottom layer of Deluxe Reversible Rack in the lower position. Place apples on top of rack, then place rack in the pot.
4. Close the lid with valve is in the seal position and move the slider to pressure. Cook on high for 7 minutes. Select DELAYED RELEASE and set time for 5 mins. Select Start/Stop to begin cooking.
5. Move slider to Air Fry/HOB to unlock the lid, then carefully open it. Remove apples to serving plates. Serve warm.

APPLE & RHUBARB CRISP

(🕐) **30 Minutes** (👤) **Serves 8**

Ingredients:

- 8 medium apples, cored, cut into chunks
- 500g rhubarb, cut into chunks
- 1 Tbsp lemon juice

Topping
- 200g plain flour
- 150g butter, cubed
- 110g brown sugar
- 130g porridge oats
- 1 tsp ground nutmeg,
- 1 tsp ground cinnamon,

Steps:

1. In a 20x20cm baking dish or tin, add the apples, rhubarb, lemon juice, and mix.
2. In a mixing bowl, add all topping ingredients and mix. Add topping over apple mixture. Cover with foil.
3. Add 250ml water to bottom of Ninja Foodi. Place bottom layer of Deluxe Reversible Rack in the lower position. Place the cake tin on top of rack, then place rack in the ninja pot.
4. Close the lid with valve is in the seal position and move the slider to COMBI-STEAM. Select Steam & Bake set temperature to 180°C/355°F, and time to 17 minutes. Select Start/Stop to begin cooking.
5. When cooking is complete, remove from ninja foodi. Serve with custard or ice cream.

FUDGE

(🕐) **3 Hour** (👤) **Serves 10**

Ingredients:

- 100g sugar
- 80ml water
- 110g butter, room temperature & cubed
- 350g chocolate chips
- 100g dried milk powder
- 1 tsp vanilla essence

Steps:

1. In your Ninja Foodi, add sugar and water and stir.
2. Close the lid with valve is in the seal position and move the slider to pressure. Cook on high for 11 minutes. Use the arrows to select PRESSURE RELEASE and select QUICK RELEASE. Select Start/Stop to begin cooking.
3. Open lid, add the butter, chocolate, milk powder, and vanilla to ninja and stir until melted and combined.
4. Pour/spoon the mixture into a lined 22×12 cm (2-lb) loaf tin and let it cool for 40 minutes, then transfer to fridge for 3 hours to set.
5. Lift from the tin, then cut into squares.

FLAPJACKS

🕐 30 Minutes   👤 Serves 8

Ingredients:

- 250g rolled oats
- 250 g unsalted butter
- 200g light brown sugar
- 2 tbsp golden syrup

Steps:

1. Grease 20-cm cake tin.
2. In a saucepan over low heat, add butter, golden syrup and sugar . Stir until all milted and combined.
3. In a bowl add oats. Pour sugar/butter mixture over oats, mix until all combined, then transfer mixture into the greased cake tin. Press down until flat.
4. Place bottom layer of Deluxe Reversible Rack in the lower position. Place the cake tin on top of rack, then place rack in the ninja pot.
5. Close lid and move the slider to AIR FRY/HOB. Select AIR FRY and set temperature to 185° C/365° F. Set time for 12 minutes. Press START/STOP to begin cooking.
6. Remove the lid and the cake tin. Place on a cooling rack. Let cool and then cut. Serve.

BUTTERSCOTCH PUDDING

🕐 1½ Hours   👤 Serves 3

Ingredients:

- 3 egg yolks, whisked
- 70g brown sugar
- 240ml double cream
- 2 tsp vanilla essence
- 60ml water
- pinch of salt

Steps:

1. In saucepan over medium heat, add water and sugar and bring to a boil. Simmer for 3 minutes then remove from heat and add 240ml double cream. Stir then whisk in the egg a little at a time constantly whisking. Add 2 tsp vanilla essence and salt. Stir.
2. Divide mixture between 3 ramekins.
3. Add 250ml water to bottom of Ninja Foodi. Place bottom layer of Deluxe Reversible Rack in the lower position. Place the ramekins on top of rack, then place rack in the ninja pot.
4. Close the lid with valve is in the seal position and move the slider to pressure. Cook on high for 6 minutes. Let pressure release naturally. Select Start/Stop to begin cooking.
5. Transfer pudding to refrigerator until set. Serve.

DRIED FIGS BREAD PUDDING

🕐 45 Minutes   👤 Serves 10

Ingredients:

- 8 slices white bread, cubed
- 2 tbsp butter, melted
- 1 tsp cinnamon
- 80g dried figs, raisins or berries, chopped
- 3 large eggs
- 70g caster sugar

- 1 tsp vanilla essence
- ¼ tsp salt
- 300ml milk
- ¼ tsp nutmeg
- 240ml water

Steps:

1. Grease a 20-cm cake tin with butter/cooking spray. Set aside.
2. In a large bowl, add bread cubes, butter, cinnamon, and raisins. Pour into prepared pan.
3. In the same bowl, add eggs, sugar, nutmeg, vanilla, salt and milk. Mix until combined and pour over bread mixture. Cover the cake tin with foil.
4. Add 250ml water to bottom of Ninja Foodi. Place bottom layer of Deluxe Reversible Rack in the lower position. Place the cake tin on top of rack, then place rack in the ninja pot.
5. Close the lid with valve is in the seal position and move the slider to COMBI-STEAM. Select Steam & Bake set temperature to 180°C/355°F, and time to 35 minutes. Select Start/Stop to begin cooking.
6. Open lid. Remove foil from tin and invert bread pudding onto a flat plate. Allow to cool completely then serve.

STRAWBERRY SCONES

🕐 30 Minutes 👤 Serves 3

Ingredients:

- 120g plain flour
- ½ tbsp baking powder
- 60g unsalted butter, cold & cut into small cubes
- 60ml double cream
- 1 large egg
- 1/8 tsp salt
- 4 tbsp caster sugar, divided
- 2 strawberries cubed

Glaze
- 130g icing sugar
- 2 tbsp water or milk

Steps:

1. In a large bowl, add flour, baking powder, salt and sugar, mix until combined . Mash butter gently into flour and sugar mixture. Don't over mix. until like sand texture.
2. Add the egg and the double cream and mix until it forms a dough. Transfer dough to a floured surface and form into a round. Add strawberry pieces and push them into the dough.
3. Grease 20-cm round baking tin and place scone dough. Brush dough with butter.
4. Add 250ml water to bottom of Ninja Foodi. Place bottom layer of Deluxe Reversible Rack in the lower position. Place the baking tin on top of rack, then place rack in the ninja pot.
5. Close the lid with valve is in the seal position and move the slider to COMBI-STEAM. Select Steam & Bake set temperature to 180°C/355°F, and time to 13 minutes. Select Start/Stop to begin cooking.
6. When cooking is complete, Transfer scones in a cooling rack.
7. In a bowl, add glaze ingredients and mix until combined. Drizzle the glaze on the scones and serve.

RICE PUDDING

🕐 30 Minutes 👤 Serves 4

Ingredients:

- 220g Arborio rice, rinsed
- 1 litre milk
- 100g sugar
- 1 cinnamon stick
- 1 tsp vanilla essence
- 40g unsalted butter

Steps:

1. Add all ingredients into Ninja Foodi (except butter). Stir until all combined.
2. Close the lid with valve is in the seal position and move the slider to pressure. Cook on high for 15 minutes. Select DELAYED RELEASE and set time for 10 mins. Select Start/Stop to begin cooking.
3. Move slider to Air Fry/HOB to unlock the lid, then carefully open it. Remove the cinnamon stick.
4. Mix the butter into pudding. Serve.

APPLE BREAD PUDDING

🕐 30 Minutes 👤 Serves 8

Ingredients:

- 350g cubed bread any type.
- 3 large eggs
- 600ml milk
- 375g brown sugar
- 1 tsp vanilla essence
- ½ tsp cinnamon
- ½ tsp nutmeg
- 2 medium apples peeled and chopped
- 80g raisins

Steps:

1. In a bowl, add eggs, milk, brown sugar, vanilla, cinnamon and nutmeg. Whisk.
2. In another bowl, add apples, raisins and bread. Pour liquid mixture over bread/apple mixture.
3. Pour mixture into 20cm round pan, then cover with foil, sealing edges.
4. Add 360ml water to bottom of Ninja Foodi. Place bottom layer of Deluxe Reversible Rack in the lower position. Place the pan on top of rack, then place rack in the pot.
5. Close the lid with valve is in the seal position and move the slider to COMBI-STEAM. Select Steam & Bake set temperature to 170°C/335°F, and time to 20 minutes. Select Start/Stop to begin cooking.
6. After time is up, remove bread pudding from the Ninja Foodi. Remove foil and allow to cool. Serve.

LEMON CURD PIE

🕐 1 Hour   👤 Serves 6

Ingredients:

Pie Crust:
- 180g plain flour
- ½ tsp salt
- 115g butter or lard, cold & cubed
- 3 tbsp iced water

Filling:
- 300g caster sugar
- 4 small lemons , juiced and zested
- 4 large eggs
- 3 tbsp plain flour
- ¼ tsp salt
- 4 tbsp unsalted butter ,melted
- 1 tsp vanilla

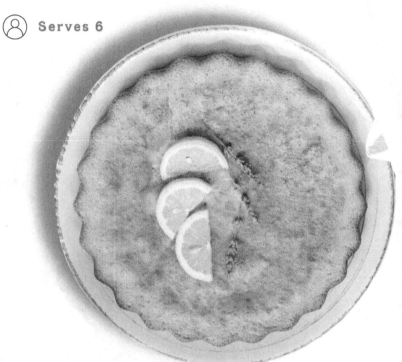

Steps:

1. In a food processor, add flour, butter and salt. Pulse until mixture resembles large crumbs.
2. Remove food processor lid and gradually drizzle in water while pulsing, until mixture starts to form a ball and holds together. Don't over mix.
3. Transfer dough onto lightly floured surface. Knead until dough holds together without cracks. Don't over-knead. Then flatten into a 2.5-cm circle. Wrap in cling-film, refrigerate for 30 mins.
4. Remove dough from refrigerator and let it sit for 5 minutes. Sprinkle a large piece of baking paper with a little flour. Add dough on baking paper and sprinkle with flour. Roll out dough into a 30-cm circle, then transfer dough into a 22-cm quiche tin. Press down and trim the edges.
5. Top with baking paper, Fill with dried beans. Place quiche pan on the Ninja Foodi middle rack.
6. Close lid and move the slider to AIR FRY/HOB. Select AIR FRY and set temperature to 190° C/375° F. Set time for 15 minutes. Press START/STOP to begin cooking.
7. In a large bowl, add all filling ingredients and whisk until combined and smooth. Pour into pie crust. Place quiche pan back on the Ninja Foodi middle rack.
8. Close lid and move the slider to AIR FRY/HOB. Select AIR FRY and set temperature to 190°C/375° F. Set time for 40 minutes until top is set. Press START/STOP to begin cooking.
9. Remove from Ninja Foodi and let cool completely. Place in the refrigerator to fully set. Serve.

Note: You can use store-bought pie crust and start at step 5.

VICTORIA SANDWICH

⏲ **35 minutes** 👤 **Serves 8**

Ingredients:

- 100g salted butter, softened,
- 100g caster sugar
- 2 large eggs, room temperature
- 100g self raising flour
- ¾ tsp vanilla essence
- ½ tsp baking powder
- 1 tbsp milk (if needed)

Filling:

- strawberry jam
- whipped double cream
- strawberries

Steps:

1. In a large mixing bowl, add butter and sugar, and mix using hand mixer for at least 5 minutes until pale and creamy. Add 1 egg at a time, along with 1 tbsp of flour with each egg, and mix for 1 minute between each addition. Continue to mix until light and airy. Mix in vanilla essence.

2. In a separate bowl, add remaining flour, baking powder. Add half of the flour mixture into the batter and use a large spoon to fold it in. Add remaining flour mixture and gently fold in. if its too thick, add 1 tbsp of milk.

3. Grease and line 20cm loose-bottomed sandwich tin with baking paper. Pour batter into tin.

4. Add 360ml water to bottom of Ninja Foodi. Place bottom layer of Deluxe Reversible Rack in the lower position. Place the tin on top of rack, then place rack in the pot.

5. Close the lid with valve is in the seal position and move the slider to COMBI-STEAM. Select Steam & Bake set temperature to 180°C/365°F, and time to 23 minutes. Select Start/Stop to begin cooking.

6. Use a skewer to check cake, and remove cake from Ninja Foodi. once the tester comes out clean. Let cool.

7. Slice in half, fill with strawberry jam and whipped cream.

STEAMED PUDDING

🕐 1 Hour   👤 Serves 6

Ingredients:

- 4 tbsp Golden Syrup
- 2 tbsp white breadcrumbs
- 150g soft butter
- 150g caster sugar
- ½ tsp lemon essence
- 1 tsp vanilla essence
- 2 large eggs
- 150g self-raising flour
- 4 tbsp milk

Cranberry Sauce:
- 300g fresh cranberries
- 100 g brown sugar
- 100ml water
- 2 star anise

Steps:

1. Grease a 1 litre pudding basin with butter. Put the Golden Syrup in its base then stir in the breadcrumbs.
2. In a large bowl, add butter and sugar and mix until light and fluffy. Mix in lemon essence and vanilla essence then the eggs one at a time. Fold in the flour then, mix in milk. Work with light hands and do not over mix.
3. Scoop into basin. Cover pudding with foil.
4. Add 500ml water to bottom of Ninja Foodi. Place bottom layer of Deluxe Reversible Rack in the lower position. Place the pudding basin on top of rack, then place rack in the pot.
5. Close the lid with valve is in the seal position and move the slider to pressure. Cook on high for 40 minutes. Select DELAYED RELEASE and set time for 10 mins. Select Start/Stop to begin cooking.
6. In a medium saucepan add all sauce ingredients and heat gently. Simmer for 15 minutes until. Leave aside to cool.
7. When cooking is complete. Move slider to Air Fry/HOB to unlock the lid, then carefully open it. Remove pudding and turn out onto a serving plate. Serve with cranberry sauce.

BANOFFEE PIE

⏱ **45 Minutes**   👤 **Serves 8**

Ingredients:

- 2 (375g each) tinned sweetened condensed milk
- 4 large bananas, peeled & sliced
- 2 tsp vanilla essence
- 2 tsp lemon juice
- 4 packs (375g each) digestive biscuits
- 30g butter, melted

Steps:

1. Peel the label from condensed milk tins and put into the Ninja Foodi. Pour hot water over tins until tins are fully covered with water.

2. Close the lid with valve is in the seal position and move the slider to pressure. Cook on high for 40 minutes. Use the arrows to select PRESSURE RELEASE and select QUICK RELEASE. Select Start/Stop to begin cooking.

3. Open the lid, drain water from the Ninja Foodi and replace with cold water and allow to cool for 10 minutes before opening the tins.

4. Crush biscuits with a rolling pin and then add in melted butter. Press crushed biscuits mixtures into bottom of 20cm spring form pan.

5. In a large mixing bowl, Pour caramel, add in sliced bananas, vanilla essence, and lemon juice. Mix.

6. Pour caramel and banana mixture over biscuit base and press down with a spoon. garnish with squirty cream. Chill in the fridge for at least 3 hours then serve.

APPLESAUCE

🕐 30 Minutes 👤 Serves 8

Ingredients:

- 8 large apples , peeled, cored and chopped
- 240ml water
- 1 tbsp fresh lemon juice
- ½ tsp ground cinnamon

Steps:

1. Add all ingredients to Ninja Foodi pot and stir to combine.
2. Close the lid with valve is in the seal position and move the slider to pressure. Cook on high for 8 minutes. Let pressure release naturally. Select Start/Stop to begin cooking.
3. Open lid, then puree with hand/regular blender. Transfer to a bowl and allow to cool completely.

STEWED RHUBARB

🕐 15 Minutes 👤 Serves 6

Ingredients:

- 450g rhubarb, chopped
- 150g-200g caster sugar
- ¼ tsp cinnamon
- ¼ tsp ginger
- 2 star anise
- 60ml orange juice

Steps:

1. Add all ingredients to Ninja Foodi pot.
2. Close the lid with valve is in the seal position and move the slider to pressure. Cook on high for 8 minutes. Let pressure release naturally. Select Start/Stop to begin cooking.
3. When cooking is complete, divide the mix into bowls and serve cold.

MINCEMEAT PUDDING

🕐 1 Hour   👤 Serves 6

Ingredients:

- 300g mincemeat
- 150g orange marmalade
- 250g dark brown sugar
- 60ml molasses/treacle
- 3 large eggs
- 120g butter, room temprature
- 180g plain flour
- 1 ½ tsp baking powder

- 5 tbsp milk
- 1 tsp ground cinnamon
- 1 tsp mixed spice
- ½ tsp ground cloves
- ½ tsp ground nutmeg

Steps:

1. Grease large (1.5 litre) pudding basin. Set aside.

2. In large bowl, add mincemeat, orange marmalade, treacle and spices. Mix.

3. In another bowl, add butter and sugar. Mix with hand mixer fluffy. Add eggs one at a time, while mixing. Next add milk and mix. Finally, add in flour, baking powder and mincemeat mixture, mix until combined.

4. Pour the batter into prepared basin and cover with baking paper and foil.

5. Add 250ml water to bottom of Ninja Foodi. Place bottom layer of Deluxe Reversible Rack in the lower position. Place the pudding basin on top of rack, then place rack in the ninja pot.

6. Close the lid with valve is in the seal position and move the slider to COMBI-STEAM. Select Steam & Bake set temperature to 180°C/356°F, and time to 40 minutes. Select Start/Stop to begin cooking.

7. When cooking time is complete, use a skewer to check the pudding. If it comes out clean, the pudding is ready. If not, bake for a further 5-10 minutes covering with foil. Then carefully remove and let cook slightly then serve.

BAKED BEANS

 1 ¾ Hours Serves 6

Ingredients:

- 240ml water
- 1 onion, diced
- 2 tsp smoked paprika
- 1 tsp garlic powder
- 1 tsp onion powder
- 450g dried haricot beans, rinsed (not soaked)
- 1 litre vegetable broth
- 50ml golden syrup
- 60g tomato concentrate/puree
- 60ml apple cider vinegar
- 2 tbsp mustard
- 2 bay leaves
- Salt & pepper to taste

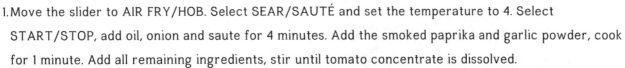

Steps:

1. Move the slider to AIR FRY/HOB. Select SEAR/SAUTÉ and set the temperature to 4. Select START/STOP, add oil, onion and saute for 4 minutes. Add the smoked paprika and garlic powder, cook for 1 minute. Add all remaining ingredients, stir until tomato concentrate is dissolved.
2. Close the lid with valve is in the seal position and move the slider to pressure. Cook on high for 78 minutes.Select DELAYED RELEASE and set time for 20 mins. Select Start/Stop to begin cooking.
3. Open lid and remove bay leaves and adjust seasoning.

JACKET POTATO

 30 Minutes Serves 5

Ingredients:

- 5 medium Maris Piper, King Edward potatoes, poked with a fork
- 250ml water

Steps:

1. Add water to inside pot of the Ninja Foodi.
2. Place bottom layer of Deluxe Reversible Rack in the lower position. Place potatoes on the rack, then place rack in the ninja.
3. Close the lid with valve is in the seal position and move the slider to pressure. Cook on high for 13 minutes. Then Use the arrows to select PRESSURE RELEASE and select QUICK RELEASE. Select Start/Stop to begin cooking.
4. Open lid, Rub the potato skin with oil and salt. Place potatoes back on the rack.
5. Close the lid with valve is in the seal position and move the slider to COMBI-STEAM. Select Steam & Bake set temperature to 180°C/365°F, and time to 8 minutes. Select Start/Stop to begin cooking.
6. Cut potatoes in the center to start cooling, then serve them with your favorite topping.

POTATO GRATIN

⏱ 20 Minutes 👤 Serves 4

Ingredients:

- 5 medium potatoes, peeled & thinly sliced
- 240ml chicken stock
- 1 onion, finely chopped
- 4 garlic cloves, minced
- salt and pepper to taste
- 120ml double cream
- 100g grated cheese (cheddar & Old Winchester)
- Salt & pepper to taste

Steps:

1. Add chicken stock, potatoes, onion, garlic, salt & pepper to the Ninja Foodi.
2. Close the lid with valve is in the seal position and move the slider to pressure. Cook on high for Zero minutes. Then Use the arrows to select PRESSURE RELEASE and select QUICK RELEASE. Select Start/Stop to begin cooking.
3. Open lid, add cheese and double cream. Stir gently. Top with more cheese.
4. Close lid and move the slider to AIR FRY/HOB. Select AIR FRY and set temperature to 190° C/375° F. Set time for 15-18 minutes until golden brown. Press START/STOP to begin cooking.
5. Let cool for 10 minutes before serving.

KEDGEREE

⏱ 25 Minutes 👤 Serves 6

Ingredients:

- 500g basmati rice
- 3 tbsp oil
- 1 large onion, chopped
- 2 tbsp curry powder
- 450g smoked haddock
- 600ml boiling water
- 6 eggs
- Salt & pepper to taste

Steps:

1. Move the slider to AIR FRY/HOB. Select SEAR/SAUTÉ and set the temperature to 4. Select START/STOP, add oil, onion and saute until soft. Add the curry powder, salt and pepper. Add rice and water. Stir, scrapping the pot bottom. Place bottom layer of Deluxe Reversible Rack in the mid position. then place rack in the ninja. Place eggs on the rack.
2. Close the lid with valve is in the seal position and move the slider to pressure. Cook on high for 4 minutes. Select DELAYED RELEASE and set time for 4 mins. Select Start/Stop to begin cooking.
3. Remove eggs and place in a bowl of iced water for a minute, Peel the eggs and cut in quarters.
4. Stir kedgeree . Serve with eggs.

SPINACH AND MUSHROOM QUICHE

 1 Hour Serves 6

Ingredients:

- 4 large eggs, whisked
- 120g Cheddar cheese, shredded
- 250g frozen spinach, thawed & drained
- 1 small onions, finely chopped
- 2 cloves garlic, minced

- 250g mushrooms, sliced
- 60g Fettle/fetta cheese
- Salt & pepper to taste
- 300ml milk
- 4 slices white bread, cubed

Steps:

1. Move the slider to AIR FRY/HOB. Select SEAR/SAUTÉ and set the temperature to 4. Select START/STOP, add oil, mushrooms, garlic, salt and saute until no water remain in pot. Stop SAUTÉ.

2. Grease 22-cm pie dish, transfer mushroom mixture into pie dish along with fettle, bread and spinach.

3. In a large bowl, add eggs, cheese, milk, salt & pepper. Whisk until combined. Pour into pie dish.

4. Add 300ml water to Ninja Foodi, scrapping any stuck pieces on the bottom. Place bottom layer of Deluxe Reversible Rack in the lower position. Place pie dish on top of rack, then place rack in the ninja.

5. Close the lid with valve is in the seal position and move the slider to COMBI-STEAM. Select Steam & Bake set temperature to 175°C/350°F, and time to 45 minutes. Select Start/Stop to begin cooking.

6. Slice and serve.

BROCCOLI AND CHEESE OMELET

30 Minutes  Serves 3

Ingredients:

- 6 large eggs
- Salt & pepper to taste
- 225g broccoli florets
- 3 scallion, chopped
- 60g grated cheddar cheese

Steps:

1. In a large bowl, add all ingredients and whisk until combined . Grease a 20-cm tin, then pour egg mixture into the tin. Place bottom layer of Deluxe Reversible Rack in the lower position. Place tin on top of rack, then place rack in the ninja.

2. Close lid and move the slider to AIR FRY/HOB. Select AIR FRY and set temperature to 180° C/356° F. Set time for 25 minutes until golden brown. Press START/STOP to begin cooking.

3. Removve from Ninja and serve.

BREAKFAST HASH BROWNS CASSEROLE

Ingredients:

 1 Hour   Serves 6

- 1 (900g) bag frozen hash browns/mini hash browns
- 450g ground turkey sausage
- 6 large eggs
- 2 tbsp heavy cream

- ½ tsp dried thyme
- ½ tsp garlic powder
- salt & pepper to taste
- 120g shredded gouda cheese

Steps:

1. Move the slider to AIR FRY/HOB. Select SEAR/SAUTÉ and set the temperature to HI-4. Select START/STOP, add sausage and cook until browned. Transfer sausage into a bowl.
2. Add 300ml water to Ninja Foodi and scrape stuck bits on bottom of inner pot.
3. In a bowl, add eggs, milk, salt and pepper. Whisk until combined.
4. Grease a 18cm baking dish. Add hash browns then sprinkle sausage over hash browns. Finally pour egg mixture over sausage and hash browns. Top with cheese and cover with foil.
5. Place bottom layer of Deluxe Reversible Rack in the lower position. Place the baking dish on top of rack, then place rack in the Ninja.
6. Close the lid with valve is in the seal position and move the slider to COMBI-STEAM. Select Steam & Bake set temperature to 177°C/350°F, and time to 55 minutes. Select Start/Stop to begin cooking. Serve.

BREAKFAST EGGS

Ingredients:

 50 Minutes Serves 8

- 1 tbsp.olive oil
- 8 eggs
- 2 tsp. dried oregano
- 100ml milk
- Salt & pepper to taste

- 60g chopped spinach
- 1 2 onion, chopped
- 1 tomato, chopped
- 1 tsp. minced garlic
- 120g crumbled goat cheese

Steps:

1. In a large bowl, add all ingredients and whisk until combined .
2. Grease a 23-cm tin, then pour egg mixture into the tin.
3. Place bottom layer of Deluxe Reversible Rack in the lower position. Place tin on top of rack, then place rack in the ninja.
4. Close lid and move the slider to AIR FRY/HOB. Select AIR FRY and set temperature to 180° C/356° F. Set time for 35 minutes until golden brown. Press START/STOP to begin cooking.
5. Remove from Ninja and serve.

BREAKFAST VEGETABLE OMELET

Ingredients:

🕐 50 Minutes 👤 Serves 3

- 1 tbsp. olive oil
- 120ml heavy cream
- 10 eggs
- 1 tsp. minced garlic
- salt & pepper to taste
- 1 green bell pepper, chopped
- 80g chopped broccoli
- 80g chopped cauliflower
- 1 scallion , white and green parts, chopped
- 120g goat cheese, crumbled

Steps:

1. In a mixing bowl, add heavy cream, eggs, garlic, pepper and salt, whisk. Then add bell pepper, broccoli, cauliflower and scallion, stir. Pour mixture into a greased 20-cm baking dish . Sprinkle the goat cheese over mixture.

2. Place bottom layer of Deluxe Reversible Rack in the lower position. Place baking dish on top of rack, then place rack in the ninja.

3. Close lid and move the slider to AIR FRY/HOB. Select AIR FRY and set temperature to 180° C/356° F. Set time for 30-40 minutes. Press START/STOP to begin cooking. Serve.

EGG AND HASH BROWNS CASSEROLE

Ingredients:

🕐 1 Hour 👤 Serves 4

- 1 (800g) package hash browns/mini hash browns
- 180g salami, diced
- 4 scallion, chopped
- 4 tbsp plain flour
- 100g grated Old Winchester
- 200g gouda cheese, shredded
- 100g shredded cheddar cheese
- 12 eggs
- 240ml milk
- salt and pepper to taste

Steps:

1. In a greased cake tin/baking dish that will fit inside Ninja Foodi , layer ⅓ of hash browns, salami, scallion and cheeses. Repeat twice.

2. In a mixing bowl, combine egg, flour, milk salt and pepper; pour the mixture over the ingredients in tin. top with shredded cheddar cheese

3. Place bottom layer of Deluxe Reversible Rack in the lower position. Place baking dish on top of rack, then place rack in the ninja.

4. Close lid and move the slider to AIR FRY/HOB. Select AIR FRY and set temperature to 176° C/350° F. Set time for 45-50 minutes. Press START/STOP to begin cooking. Serve.

DRIED FRUITS PORRIDGE

🕐 15 Minutes 👤 Serves 6

Ingredients:

- 450ml water
- 450ml milk
- 320g steel cut oats/coarse oats
- 50g raisins
- 50g dried cherries
- 50g dried figs
- ½ tsp salt
- 5 tbsp brown sugar
- 1 tbsp butter
- ½ tsp vanilla essence
- ¼ tsp ground cinnamon
- 3 tbsp toasted chopped pecans

Steps:

1. Add water, milk, oats, raisins, cherries, figs and salt in Ninja Foodi.
2. Close the lid with valve is in the seal position and move the slider to pressure. Cook on high for 4 minutes. Use the arrows to select PRESSURE RELEASE and select QUICK RELEASE. Select Start/Stop to begin cooking.
3. Open lid, stir and add sugar, butter, vanilla, and cinnamon. Stir and serve topped with pecans.

BAKED OATS

🕐 17 Minutes 👤 Serves 4

Ingredients:

- 1 large Banana
- 80g rolled oats
- 2 tbsp golden syrup
- 2 tsp vanilla essence
- 2 tsp baking powder
- 2 large eggs
- 80g milk
- 1 tsp ground cinnamon or nutmeg
- Blueberries or your favorite fruits

Steps:

1. Grease 4 ramekins and set aside. Add all ingredients into the blender. Blend till smooth.
2. Add oats mixture to ramekins and top with fruits.
3. Add 300ml water to Ninja Foodi. Place bottom layer of Deluxe Reversible Rack in the lower position. Place loaf tin on top of rack, then place rack in the ninja.
4. Close the lid with valve is in the seal position and move the slider to COMBI-STEAM. Select Steam & Bake set temperature to 165°C/330°F, and time to 15 minutes. Select Start/Stop to begin cooking.

NUTS SPICED PORRIDGE

🕐 15 Minutes 👤 Serves 4

Ingredients:

- 160g steel cut oats/coarse oats
- 1 tbsp butter
- ¼ tsp turmeric powder
- ½ tsp allspice or Mixed spice
- 2 tbsp golden syrup
- 200g dried figs
- 200g dried apricots
- 200ml water
- 300ml coconut water
- 120ml half cream
- ½ tsp salt
- Chopped nuts for serving

Steps:

1. Add all ingredients in Ninja Foodi.
2. Close the lid with valve is in the seal position and move the slider to pressure. Cook on high for 3 minutes. Use the arrows to the left of the display to select PRESSURE RELEASE and select QUICK RELEASE. Select Start/Stop to begin cooking.
3. Serve with chopped nuts.

APPLE PORRIDGE

🕐 30 Minutes 👤 Serves 6

Ingredients:

- 250g steel cut oats/coarse oats
- 720ml milk
- 450ml water
- 2 medium apples, shredded
- 1 tsp cinnamon
- ⅛ tsp salt
- 2 tsp vanilla essence

Steps:

1. Add all ingredients in Ninja Foodi (except vanilla essence).
2. Close the lid with valve is in the seal position and move the slider to pressure. Cook on high for 6 minutes. Select DELAYED RELEASE and set time for 10 mins. Select Start/Stop to begin cooking.
3. Open lid and add vanilla essence. Serve with chopped apples, toasted pecans, and additional cinnamon.

WHITE BREAD LOAF

Ingredients:

(L) 30 Minutes (8) Serves 6

- 190g plain flour
- 1 tsp Bicarbonate of soda
- 1 tsp baking powder
- A pinch of salt
- 4 tbsp butter, cut into pieces
- A pinch of grated nutmeg
- 180ml buttermilk

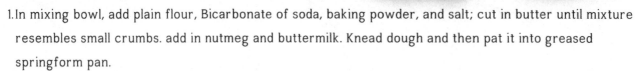

Steps:

1. In mixing bowl, add plain flour, Bicarbonate of soda, baking powder, and salt; cut in butter until mixture resembles small crumbs. add in nutmeg and buttermilk. Knead dough and then pat it into greased springform pan.
2. Add 360ml water to bottom of Ninja Foodi. Place bottom layer of Deluxe Reversible Rack in the lower position. Place the tin on top of rack, then place rack in the Ninja.
3. Close the lid with valve is in the seal position and move the slider to COMBI-STEAM. Select STEAM BREAD set temperature to 195°C/390°F, and time to 25-30 minutes. Select Start/Stop to begin cooking.
4. Remove the tin to a rack and let cool. Serve.

SODA BREAD

Ingredients:

(L) 50 Minutes (8) Serves 10

- 350g self-raising flour
- 1 ½ tsp bicarbonate of soda
- ½ tsp salt
- 150g dried fruit mix
- 300ml buttermilk
- 4 tsp caster sugar
- 1 egg, beaten

Steps:

1. In a mixing bowl, add flour, bicarbonate of soda, salt, sugar and dried fruit. mix. Add buttermilk and stir. Bring together with hands then transfer dough to floured surface and form into a round loaf shape. Slash the top with a sharp knife.
2. Grease a cake tin or pie dish that will fit in your Ninja Foodi. Transfer the dough to the prepared tin/dish. Brush loaf top with beaten egg.
3. Add 360ml water to bottom of Ninja Foodi. Place bottom layer of Deluxe Reversible Rack in the lower position. Place the tin on top of rack, then place rack in the Ninja.
4. Close the lid with valve is in the seal position and move the slider to COMBI-STEAM. Select STEAM BREAD set temperature to 200°C/395°F, and time to 40-45 minutes. Select Start/Stop to begin cooking.
5. Remove the tin to a rack and let cool. Serve.

HOT CROSS BUNS

🕐 **2 Hours** 👤 **Serves 16**

Ingredients:

- 180ml warm milk
- 2 tsp vanilla essence
- 1 large egg, room temperature
- 360g plain flour
- 70g caster sugar
- 1 tsp salt
- 3 tsp active dry yeast

- 60g butter, softened & cut into pieces
- 1 ½ tsp ground cinnamon
- 100g currants
- 1 large egg yolk mixed with 2 tbsp water

For the Icing:
- 200g icing sugar
- 2 tbsp milk
- ½ tsp vanilla essence

Steps:

1. In large bowl add milk, vanilla and egg, whisk until combined. Add flour, sugar, salt, yeast, and butter. Mix until combined. Transfer to floured surface and knead, add currants and cinnamon in, knead for 10 mins until smooth and elastic. Cover and let dough rise in warm place for 45 minutes.
2. Shape dough into 16 balls and transfer balls into a greased 23-cm square baking tin. Cover with a cloth and let rise for 40 minutes. Brush buns tops with egg yolk mixture.
3. Add 360ml water to bottom of Ninja Foodi. Place bottom layer of Deluxe Reversible Rack in the lower position. Place the tin on top of rack, then place rack in the Ninja.
4. Close the lid with valve is in the seal position and move the slider to COMBI-STEAM. Select STEAM BREAD set temperature to 177°C/350°F, and time to 25 minutes. Select Start/Stop to begin cooking.
5. Remove the tin to a rack and let cool.
6. In a bowl, add icing sugar, milk and vanilla; stir until smooth. Add milk or more sugar, as needed. Drizzle crosses over buns.

BUTTERMILK BISCUITS

 30 Minutes Serves 6

Ingredients:

- 240g plain flour
- 1 tsp Bicarbonate of soda
- 2 tsp baking powder
- 1 tsp salt
- 100g frozen butter, grated
- A pinch of grated nutmeg
- 180ml buttermilk

Steps:

1. In mixing bowl, add plain flour, Bicarbonate of soda, baking powder, and salt; add in butter and mix until mixture resembles small crumbs. Make a well in the center, pour buttermilk and mix until just combined. Transfer dough into a floured surface. Roll into rectangle. Cut into 12 round biscuits.
2. Place biscuits on Cook & Crisp Basket. Brush with buttermilk. Place basket in Ninja. (you may need to work in batches)
3. Close the lid and move the slider to AIR FRY/HOB. Select AIR FRY, set the temperature to 190°C/375°F, and set the time to 15-20 minutes. Press START/STOP to begin cooking.

LEMONADE SCONES

 30 Minutes Serves 16

Ingredients:

- 500g self-raising flour
- 70g caster sugar
- 300ml heavy cream
- 180ml lemonade
- 1 tsp vanilla essence
- Milk, for brushing

Steps:

1. In a large mixing bowl, add flour, sugar, cream, lemonade and vanilla. Gently mix until dough just comes together.
2. Transfer dough onto a floured surface. Knead until just smooth. Press the dough to a 2.5cm thick round. Cut out 5.5cm scones. Repeat to make 16 scones.
3. Place scones on Cook & Crisp Basket. Brush top with milk. (you may need to cook in batches).
4. Close the lid and move the slider to AIR FRY/HOB. Select AIR FRY, set the temperature to 160°C/320°F, and set the time to 12-15 minutes. Press START/STOP to begin cooking.
5. Serve warm.

BANANA BREAD

🕐 50 Minutes 👤 Serves 6

Ingredients:

- 3 medium ripe bananas
- 80g butter, melted
- 150g caster sugar
- 2 large eggs
- 1 tsp vanilla essence
- 240g plain flour

- 1 tsp Bicarbonate of soda
- 1 tsp baking powder
- ½ tsp salt
- 1 tsp cinnamon

Steps:

1. In a large mixing bowl, add bananas, butter. Mash with a fork, then add sugar and mix until combined. Add all remaining ingredients until all combined.
2. Grease a 20x8-cm (2lb) loaf tin. Pour batter into loaf tin.
3. Add 300ml water to Ninja Foodi. Place bottom layer of Deluxe Reversible Rack in the lower position. Place loaf tin on top of rack, then place rack in the ninja.
4. Close the lid with valve is in the seal position and move the slider to COMBI-STEAM. Select Steam & Bake set temperature to 175°C/350°F, and time to 45 minutes. Select Start/Stop to begin cooking.
5. Remove from Ninja and let cool in the tin for a few minutes. Then remove from tin, let cool completely before serving. Slice and serve.

EGGY BREAD CASSEROLE

🕐 40 Minutes 👤 Serves 6

Ingredients:

- 180g cubed bread
- 6 eggs
- 450ml milk
- ½ tsp salt
- 1 ½ tsp. ground cinnamon
- ¼ tsp ground nutmeg

- 60ml golden syrup
- 100g chopped nuts
- 70g butter, cubed

Steps:

1. In a large mixing bowl, add eggs, milk, salt, cinnamon, nutmeg, and golden syrup, mix.
2. Grease a deep baking/pudding dish that will fit in your Ninja Foodi. Add cubed bread, then pour in milk/egg mixture. Press all the bread pieces slightly into mixture. Add pecans on top. Then sprinkle sugar and cinnamon on top. Finally add butter evenly on top of the sugar.
3. Add 300ml water to Ninja Foodi. Place bottom layer of Deluxe Reversible Rack in the lower position. Place dish on top of rack, then place rack in the ninja.
4. Close the lid with valve is in the seal position and move the slider to COMBI-STEAM. Select Steam & Bake set temperature to 190°C/375°F, and time to 25 minutes. Select Start/Stop to begin cooking.

BUBBLE & SQUEAK

🕐 40 Minutes   👤 Serves 6

Ingredients:

- 1 kg maris piper potatoes, peeled & cut into 2.5cm pieces
- 500g mixed vegetables (carrots, cabbage, swede, turnips), peeled & cut into 2.5cm pieces. or you can use just cabbage
- 1 onion, finely chopped
- 500ml water
- Salt & pepper to taste.

Steps:

1. Put the potatoes, vegetables, water and salt in Ninja Foodi.
2. Close the lid with valve is in the seal position and move the slider to pressure. Cook on high for 10 minutes. Use the arrows to select PRESSURE RELEASE and select QUICK RELEASE. Select Start/Stop to begin cooking. Move slider to Air Fry/HOB to unlock the lid, then carefully open it.
3. Drain vegetables and transfer to a bowl, leave to dry for 6 minutes.
4. Season vegetable/potatoes with salt and pepper, then mash. Add onion and mix.
5. Roll mixture into balls, flatten slightly. Place on Cook & Crisp Basket. Brush with oil. Place basket in Ninja.
6. Close the lid and move the slider to AIR FRY/HOB. Select AIR FRY, set the temperature to 190°C/375°F, and set the time to 25 minutes. Press START/STOP to begin cooking. flip and AIR FRY for 5 minutes.

COURGETTE FRIES

🕐 18 Minutes   👤 Serves 6

Ingredients:

- 2 medium courgette, (cut into fries)
- 180g plain flour
- 2 eggs, (beaten)
- 250g breadcrumbs
- 60g grated Old Winchester/Parmesan
- Salt & pepper to taste

Steps:

1. In a medium mixing bowl, add flour. In another mixing bowl, add beaten eggs. In a 3rd bowl, mix breadcrumbs, cheese and season with salt & pepper.
2. Dip each courgette fries in the flour, shake off excess. Then coat with eggs. Finally coat with breadcrumb mixture.
3. Place on Cook & Crisp Basket. Brush with oil. Place basket in Ninja.
4. Close the lid and move the slider to AIR FRY/HOB. Select AIR FRY, set the temperature to 190°C/375°F, and set the time to 8 minutes. Press START/STOP to begin cooking. flip and AIR FRY for 5 minutes.

SAUSAGE ROLLS

 Ingredients: ⏰ 40 Minutes 👤 Serves 4

- 2 tbsp oil
- 1 onion, finely chopped

- 6 higher-welfare sausages
- 4 tbsp breadcrumbs
- 250g puff pastry
- 1 egg mixed with 4 tbsp milk

Steps:

1. Move the slider to AIR FRY/HOB. Select SEAR/SAUTÉ and set the temperature to low. Select START/STOP, add oil, and cook onion until soft and golden.
2. With a sharp knife, cut skin of sausages and take meat out. Add it in bowl with sauteed and breadcrumbs. Then mix well with hands until combined.
3. Roll pastry out into a big rectangle on a floured surface and cut it lengthways to 2 long rectangles. Roll the meat into sausage shapes and lay it in the centre of each rectangle.
4. Brush pastry with egg/water mixter, then fold one side of the pastry over, wrapping the filling inside. Press down with edge of a spoon to seal. Cut into pieces and brush with egg wash.
5. Spray Cook & Crisp Basket with cooking spray. Add sausage rolls on basket in a single layer. Place basket in Ninja Foodi.
6. Close the lid and move the slider to AIR FRY/HOB. Select AIR FRY, set the temperature to 165°C/325°F, and set the time to 25 minutes. Press START/STOP to begin cooking.

FISH CAKES

⏰ 40 Minutes 👤 Serves 4

 Ingredients:

- 500g skinless cod/haddock fillets, chopped
- 250g peeled & grated potatoes

- 4 tbsp plain flour
- 2 tbsp dill & parsley, chopped
- Salt & pepper to taste

Steps:

1. In a large bowl, add chopped fish, grated potatoes, dill and flour. Season with salt & pepper. Mix until combined. Shape into 8 patties, then let rest in the fridge for 30 minutes.
2. Spray Cook & Crisp Basket with cooking spray. Add patties on basket in a single layer coat with cooking spray. Place basket in pot
3. Close the lid and move the slider to AIR FRY/HOB. Select AIR FRY, set the temperature to 190°C/375°F, and set the time to 5 minutes. Press START/STOP to begin cooking. Flip and AIR FRY for more 4 minutes.

POTATO MASH

⏱ 10 Minutes 👤 Serves 8

Ingredients:

- 1 kg potatoes, peeled and quartered
- 60g butter
- 60ml double cream/milk
- 240ml water
- salt & pepper to taste

Steps:

1. Put the potatoes, water and salt in Ninja Foodi.
2. Close the lid with valve is in the seal position and move the slider to pressure. Cook on high for 10 minutes. Use the arrows tto select PRESSURE RELEASE and select QUICK RELEASE. Select Start/Stop to begin cooking.
3. Move slider to Air Fry/HOB to unlock the lid, then carefully open it.
4. Drain and add the double cream, butter, and pepper to the Ninja Foodi.
5. Use a potato masher to mash the potatoes to the desired consistency. (add more salt and double cream if necessary).

YORKSHIRE PUDDING

⏱ 30 Minutes 👤 Serves 7

Ingredients:

- 80g plain flour
- ¼ teaspoon salt
- 2 large eggs, room temperature
- 120ml warm milk
- 6 tsp oil or lard

Steps:

1. In a mixing bowl, add flour and salt. Mix, then make a well in the center. Add eggs and milk. Mix until smooth. Allow to rest for 30 minutes.
2. Add a tsp oil in each hole of 6-hole tin. Place bottom layer of Deluxe Reversible Rack in the lower position. Place tin on top of rack, then place rack in the ninja.
3. Close the lid and move the slider to AIR FRY/HOB. Select AIR FRY, set the temperature to 190°C/375°F, and set the time to 8 minutes. Press START/STOP to begin cooking.
4. Crefully remove tin from Ninja Foodi and fill each hole with pudding batter ⅓ way full, then place rack in the ninja.
5. Close the lid and move the slider to AIR FRY/HOB. Select AIR FRY, set the temperature to 190°C/375°F, and set the time to 15-18 minutes. Press START/STOP to begin cooking. Serve immediately.

CHEESE AND LEEK SOUFFLÉ

🕐 40 Minutes 👤 Serves 6

Ingredients:

- 115g unsalted butter
- 1 leek, finely sliced
- 60g plain flour
- 2 tsp Dijon/English mustard
- 300ml milk
- 100g Gouda cheese
- 4 large eggs, separated
- Salt & pepper to taste

Steps:

1. Move the slider to AIR FRY/HOB. Select SEAR/SAUTÉ and set the temperature to HI-4. Select START/STOP, add butter, leek and saute until soft. While continuously stirring, Add flour and mustard. Pour in milk and mix until thick. Season with salt & pepper.
2. Transfer mixture to a large bowl. Add egg yolks and mix until combined. Add cheese and stir.
3. In bowl, beat 4 egg whites until stiff and firm. Fold in egg whites in 2 parts into egg yolks/leek mixture.
4. Grease 6 240ml/6oz. ramekins and fill with soufflé mixture, leaving 1½-cm from top. Rinse the ninja inner pot. Add 360ml water to bottom of Ninja Foodi.
5. Place bottom layer of Deluxe Reversible Rack in lower position. Place ramekins on top of rack, then place rack in the Ninja.
6. Close the lid with valve is in the seal position and move the slider to COMBI-STEAM. Select Steam & Bake set temp. to 190°C/375°F, and time to 16 mins. Select Start/Stop to begin cooking. Serve hot.

ONION FRIED RICE

🕐 30 Minutes 👤 Serves 3

Ingredients:

- 2 tbsp oil
- 2 medium onions, finely chopped
- 375g uncooked basmati rice
- 700ml beef stock
- ¼ tsp garlic powder
- ½ tsp ground cumin
- ½ tsp dark soy sauce
- 2 eggs, beaten
- Salt & pepper to taste

Steps:

1. Add rice and stock to your Ninja Foodi inner pot.
2. Close the lid with valve is in the seal position and move the slider to pressure. Cook on high for 4 minutes. Select DELAYED RELEASE and set time for 10 mins. Select Start/Stop to begin cooking.
3. Move slider to Air Fry/HOB to unlock the lid, then carefully open it.
4. Open the lid and fluff the rice with a fork. Transfer the rice to a bowl and set aside to cool off.
5. Move the slider to AIR FRY/HOB. Select SEAR/SAUTÉ and set the temperature to HI-4. Select START/STOP, add oil, onion, once softened add garlic & saute for 1 min. Push ingredients to side of pot.
6. Add beaten egg and cook, stirring constantly, until the egg begins to set. Mix onion and egg until cooked through. Put the rice back into the Ninja Foodi and give all ingredients a good mix.
7. Turn off the Ninja Foodi. Add soy sauce and spices, mix and serve.

ROAST POTATOES

🕐 30 Minutes 👤 Serves 4

Ingredients:

- 1 kg small potatoes, halved
- 4 tbsp oil
- 1 tsp paprika
- 1 tsp garlic powder
- 1 tsp salt
- 300ml hot water

Steps:

1. Add water to your Ninja Foodi inner pot. Add Foodi Cook & Crisp basket in, add potatoes in the basket.

2. Close lid and cook on high pressure for 1 minute. Use the arrows to select PRESSURE RELEASE and select QUICK RELEASE. Select Start/Stop to begin cooking. Move slider to Air Fry/HOB to unlock the lid, then carefully open it.

3. Open lid, remove basket let potatoes dry for 15 mins. Season potatoes with paprika, garlic powder, salt and oil. mix until coated with seasoning and oil.

4. Drain water from Ninja Foodi. Add Foodi Cook & Crisp basket in, add potatoes in the basket.

5. Close the lid and move the slider to AIR FRY/HOB. Select AIR FRY, set the temperature to 200°C/395°F, and set time to 20 mins. Press START/STOP to begin cooking. Flipping halfway through cooking time.

HERBY BABY POTATOES

🕐 15 Minutes 👤 Serves 6

Ingredients:

- 1 kg baby potatoes, washed and poked with a fork
- 2 Tbsp olive oil
- 2 tsp garlic, minced
- salt & pepper to taste
- 2 tsp chives, chopped
- 1 tbsp parsley, chopped
- 60g butter, cubed
- 120ml water

Steps:

1. In your Ninja Foodi, add all ingredients except butter. Mix until combined. Add butter cubes over potatoes.

2. Close lid and cook on high pressure for 9 minutes. Use the arrows to select PRESSURE RELEASE and select QUICK RELEASE. Select Start/Stop to begin cooking. Move slider to Air Fry/HOB to unlock the lid, then carefully open it.

3. Open lid, serve hot.

CORNED BEEF

🕐 1 ½ Hours 👤 Serves 8

Ingredients:

- 2 kg corned beef
- 500ml vegetable stock
- 1 head cabbage, (cut into 8 wedges)
- 250g potatoes , (cut into wedges)
- 250g carrots, (cut into thick fries)

- 3 bay leaves
- 1 large onion, (peeled & quartered)
- Salt & pepper to taste
- 1 tsp black peppercorns
- ½ tsp anise seeds
- 8 whole cloves
- 4 cardamom pods
- 4 large bay leaves (crushed)
- 1 tbsp ground coriander
- ½ tsp ground ginger

Steps:

1. Put corned beef and stock in the Ninja foodi pot. Add water then add seasoning over beef.

2. Secure lid with valve in seal position. Cook on high pressure for 80 mins. Use the arrows to select PRESSURE RELEASE and select QUICK RELEASE. Select Start/Stop to begin cooking.

3. Remove corned beef from Ninja pot, Add potatoes, carrots and cabbage to the Ninja foodi pot.

4. Secure lid with valve in seal position. Cook on high pressure for 3 minutes. select QUICK RELEASE.

5. Open lid, Mix butter, salt & pepper, and drizzle over vegetables. Serve beef with vegetables.

POT ROAST

🕐 2 Hours 👤 Serves 8

Ingredients:

- 2 kg braising steak or pot roast
- 500ml beef stock/water
- 5 carrots, cut into chunks
- 8 potatoes, cut into chunks/ halved if small
- 6 cloves garlic, minced
- 2 large onions cut into chunks

- 1 sprig fresh rosemary
- 1 sprig fresh thyme
- Salt & pepper to taste
- 2 tbsp light brown sugar
- 2 tsp dried oregano
- 1 tsp paprika
- 2 whole bay leaves

Steps:

1. Move the slider to AIR FRY/HOB. Select SEAR/SAUTÉ and set the temperature to HI-5. Select START/STOP, add oil, braise both sides of pot roast. Remove and set aside.

2. Add in stock, onion, garlic and all seasoning. Stir and scrape the bottom of the pot. Add pot roast, potatoes and carrots.

3. Close the lid with valve is in the seal position and move the slider to pressure. Cook on high for 90 minutes. Select DELAYED RELEASE and set time for 20 mins. Select Start/Stop to begin cooking.

4. Move slider to Air Fry/HOB to unlock the lid, then carefully open it.

5. Serve hot.

COTTAGE PIE

⏱ 1 ½ Hours 👤 Serves 6

Ingredients:

- 1 tsp oil
- 1 large onion, chopped
- 2 large carrots, chopped
- 2 large field mushrooms, chopped
- 1 clove garlic, minced
- 450g beef mince
- 1 (375g) tin chopped tomato

- 1 beef stock cube
- 100 g Frozen Peas
- 2 tbsp tomato puree
- 2 tbsp cornflour mixed with 2 tbsp water

For the mash:

- 1 kg potatoes, peeled and chopped
- 200ml double cream
- 100g butter

Steps:

1. Move the slider to AIR FRY/HOB. Select SEAR/SAUTÉ and set the temperature to HI-5. Select START/STOP, add oil, onion, once softened add garlic and mince. cook until browned. Add carrots, mushrooms, tomatoes & puree, beef stock, salt & pepper. Close lid and cook on high pressure for 3 mins. Use the arrows to select PRESSURE RELEASE and select QUICK RELEASE. elect Start/Stop to begin cooking.
2. Move the slider to AIR FRY/HOB. Select SEAR/SAUTÉ and set the temperature to 4. Add cornflour mixture, simmer until thickened.
3. Grease a 23-cm deep pie dish. Add mince mixture into the pie dish. Set aside.
4. Rinse the Ninja Foodi pot. Put the potatoes, water and salt in Ninja Foodi pot.
5. Close the lid with valve is in the seal position and move the slider to pressure. Cook on high for 10 minutes. Use the arrows to select PRESSURE RELEASE and select QUICK RELEASE. Select Start/Stop to begin cooking. Move slider to Air Fry/HOB to unlock the lid, then carefully open it.
6. Drain and add the double cream, butter, and pepper to the Ninja Foodi.
7. Use a potato masher to mash the potatoes, add more salt and double cream if necessary.
8. Spread mashed potatoes evenly over the mince mixture.
9. Add 240ml water to bottom of Ninja Foodi. Place bottom layer of Deluxe Reversible Rack in the lower position. Place the dish on top of rack, then place rack in the pot.
10. Close the lid with valve is in the seal position and move the slider to COMBI-STEAM. Select Steam & Crisp set temperature to 190°C/375°F, and time to 35 minutes. Select Start/Stop to begin cooking.
11. Serve hot.

SAUSAGE AND PEPPERS

 30 Minutes **Serves 8**

Ingredients:

- 1 kg Sausages
- 500ml marinara sauce
- 4 bell peppers (sliced)
- 1 large onion, (sliced)
- Salt & pepper to taste

Steps:

1. Move the slider to AIR FRY/HOB. Select SEAR/SAUTÉ and set the temperature to 5. Select START/STOP, saute sausage in oil until browned. Add remaining ingredients.
2. Close the lid with valve is in the seal position and move the slider to pressure. Cook on high for 8 minutes. Select DELAYED RELEASE and set time for 15 mins. Select Start/Stop to begin cooking.
3. Open lid, and stir then serve.

BIRMINGHAM BALTI

Ingredients:
40 Minutes **Serves 4**

- 2 tbsp oil
- 600g lamb shoulder, cubed
- 2 onions, chopped
- 4 carrots, thickly sliced
- 3 garlic cloves, minced
- 2 tsp grated ginger
- 2 green chillies, deseeded, finely chopped

- 1 tbsp garam masala
- 2 tsp ground cumin
- Handful fresh coriander, finely chopped
- 375g tin chopped tomatoes
- 100ml lamb stock
- 375ml coconut milk

Steps:

1. Move the slider to AIR FRY/HOB. Select SEAR/SAUTÉ and set the temperature to 5. Select START/STOP, add oil, brown lamb in batches and transfer to bowl. Add more oil, cook onions and carrots until softened. Add all ingredients to Ninja Foodi pot.
2. Close lid and cook on high pressure for 25 mins. Let pressure release naturally. Select Start/Stop to begin cooking. Move slider to Air Fry/HOB to unlock the lid, then carefully open it.
3. Serve hot.

SCOTCH EGGS

🕐 **40 Minutes**   👤 **Serves 4**

Ingredients:

- 450g minced beef, (90% lean)
- 5 eggs
- 1 tsp. dried sage
- ½ tsp red chili flake
- ½ tsp garlic powder
- ½ tsp onion powder
- 60g plain flour
- 2 tbsp milk
- 60g breadcrumbs
- Salt & pepper to taste

Steps:

1. In medium saucepan over high heat. bring 1 liter of water to a boil; add 4 eggs, boil 5 minutes. Then transfer boiled eggs into a large bowl full with ice water. Peel the eggs.

2. In a large mixing bowl, add minced beef, all the spices and season with salt & pepper. Mix until all combined. Divide the minced beef into 4 portions and form into ½cm thick disks. Place the egg in the middle of each disk. Wrap the beef around each egg to fully cover the egg with beef.

3. Prepare three bowls: 1) with flour, 2) egg whisked with milk, and 3) breadcrumbs. Dredge each egg in flour, dip in egg then roll in breadcrumbs. Refrigerate Scotch eggs for 20 minutes.

4. Spray Cook & Crisp Basket with cooking spray. Add scotch eggs on basket in a single layer. Place basket in pot

5. Close the lid and move the slider to AIR FRY/HOB. Select AIR FRY, set the temperature to 190°C/375°F, and set the time to 8 minutes. Press START/STOP to begin cooking. flip and AIR FRY for more 7 minutes.

MEATBALLS & ONION GRAVY

🕐 30 Minutes   👤 Serves 4

Ingredients:

For the meatballs :
- butter for frying
- 1 kg minced beef (20% fat)
- 1 medium white onion, finely chopped
- 100ml milk
- 2 large eggs
- 60g breadcrumbs
- ½ tsp ground nutmeg
- 1 tsp ground allspice
- Salt & pepper to taste

For the gravy:
- 750ml beef stock
- 100ml double cream
- 1 large onion, finely chopped
- ½ tsp Worcestershire sauce
- ½ tsp sugar
- Salt & pepper to taste
- 2 tbsp flour mixed with 2 tbsp water

Steps:

1. In a large bowl, add onion, milk, eggs, breadcrumbs, spices. Mix until combined. Add beef and mix until combined. Refrigerate for 30 mins. Scoop into 1 ½-cm meatballs.

2. Move the slider to AIR FRY/HOB. Select SEAR/SAUTÉ and set the temperature to HI-5. Select START/STOP, add butter and brown the meatballs. Remove from Ninja Foodi and transfer to a plate.

3. Add the stock, scrape the bottom of the pot. Cancel SAUTÉ .

4. Add all remaining gravy ingredients (except flour/water mixture). Stir and add the meatballs back to the ninja pot.

5. Close the lid with valve is in the seal position and move the slider to pressure. Cook on high for 10 minutes. Use the arrows to select PRESSURE RELEASE and select QUICK RELEASE. Select Start/Stop to begin cooking.

6. Open lid and remove the meatballs and while the sauce is still hot, pour in the flour/water mixture, stirring continuously. The gravy will thicken instantly.

7. Add back the meatballs in gravy and stir. serve hot with mash.

BEEF WELLINGTON

🕐 1 ½ Hours 👤 Serves 4

Ingredients:

- 1200g beef tenderloin, 20cm long
- 2 tablespoons butter
- 350g mushrooms, finely chopped
- 1 onion, diced
- 2 tablespoons olive oil
- 12 thin slices prosciutto
- Salt & pepper to taste
- 2 garlic cloves, minced
- 2 teaspoons dried thyme
- 2 tablespoons English/Dijon mustard
- 1 egg beaten with 1 tbsp water
- 450g puff pastry

Steps:

1. Line a slow Move the slider to AIR FRY/HOB. Select SEAR/SAUTÉ and set the temperature to 5. Select START/STOP, add butter and mushrooms and onion. Cook, stirring for 3 minutes. Reduce heat 3 and continue to cook for 15 mins, stirring frequently, until mushrooms are browned and there is remaining liquid. Transfer to a bowl.

2. Set temperature to 4. Add 2 tablespoons oil to the ninja inner pot. Season beef with salt & pepper, then brown beef on all sides. Press START/STOP.Transfer to a plate, let cool slightly, then brush with mustard.

3. Place 40x40-cm sheet of cling film on top of chopping board. Place prosciutto slices on cling film make a rectangle. Spread mushroom mixture on top. Season the surface with salt & pepper and sprinkle with thyme. Roll prosciutto around beef until forms a tight log. Refrigerate for 30 minutes.

4. On a floured surface, roll the puff pastry out to 36-cm long and 23-cm wide and ½-cm thickness to cover the beef. Set the beef in the center of the pastry and fold over the longer sides, brushing with egg wash to seal. Brush all over with egg wash. Sprinkle with salt.

5. Line the Cook & Crisp Basket with baking parchment paper and place the beef, seam-side down, on top of the baking paper.

6. Add 250ml water to your Ninja Foodi inner pot. Add Foodi Cook & Crisp basket in.

7. Close the lid with valve is in the seal position and move the slider to COMBI-STEAM. Select Steam & Crisp set temperature to 165°C/325°F, and time to 30-35 minutes. Select Start/Stop to begin cooking.

8. Remove from basket and let rest for 10 minutes, then serve.

STEAK AND STILTON PIE

🕐 1 ½ Hours   👤 Serves 6

Ingredients:

For the filling:

- 1kg braising steak, cut into 4cm pieces
- 4 tbsp plain flour
- 3 tbsp oil
- 6 small shallots, halved
- 650ml beef stock
- 2 tbsp balsamic vinegar
- 2 thyme sprigs
- 1 bay leaf
- 50g Stilton, crumbled
- Salt & pepper to taste
- 2 tbsp cornflour mixed with 3 tbsp water

For the pastry:

- 225g plain flour
- 100g cold butter, diced
- 50g Stilton, crumbled
- 1 tsp dried thyme
- 5 tbsp water
- 1 egg, beaten for brushing

Steps:

1. In a large mixing bowl, add flour & salt. Mix until combined. Add the butter into the flour mixture, Mash with fork until resembles very coarse meal. Gradually add water until dough just sticks together into ball. Wrap in cling film and rest in the fridge.

2. In bowl, add flour, season with salt & pepper, mix. Add beef and mix until coated with flour.

3. Move the slider to AIR FRY/HOB. Select SEAR/SAUTÉ and set the temperature to 5. Select START/STOP, add oil. Add meat (in batches) cook until browned. Add all remaining ingredients. stir, scrapping the bottom of the pot to loose any stuck pieces.

4. Close the lid with valve is in the seal position and move the slider to pressure. Cook on high for 25 minutes.Then Use the arrows to select PRESSURE RELEASE and select QUICK RELEASE. Select Start/Stop to begin cooking.

5. Open lid, add cornflour/water mixture. Stir until thickened.

6. Grease a deep-dish pie. Transfer the pie crust into floured surface and roll it into a circle that's at least 2.5cm larger than the baking dish.

7. Pour beef mixture into the pie dish. Top with the pie crust (poke some holes in the crust top). Brush with egg.

8. Add 250ml water to bottom of Ninja Foodi. Place bottom layer of Deluxe Reversible Rack in the lower position. Place the pie dish on top of rack, then place rack in the ninja pot.

9. Close the lid with valve is in the seal position and move the slider to COMBI-STEAM. Select Steam & Bake set temperature to 190°C/375°F, and time to 20 minutes. Select Start/Stop to begin cooking.

LANCASHIRE HOT POT

🕐 1 Hour 👤 Serves 5

Ingredients:

- 2 tbsp oil
- 500g lamb, cut to bite size pieces
- 2 onions, thinly sliced
- 2 tbsp plain flour
- 500ml chicken stock
- 2 bay leaves
- 1 tbsp Worcestershire sauce
- 2 carrots, chopped
- 700g maris pipers potatoes, peeled & cut to ½-cm thick slices
- ¼ tsp dried thyme
- Melted butter
- Salt & pepper to taste

Steps:

1. Move the slider to AIR FRY/HOB. Select SEAR/SAUTÉ and set the temperature to 4 (medium-high) . Select START/STOP. Add oil, once hot. Brown lamb, remove and set aside. Add onion and carrot and saute until soft until soft, stirring occasionally.

2. Add Worcestershire sauce, and flour, sauté for 1 minute. Gradually add in stock, stirring and scrapping the bottom of the pot. Turn off SEAR/SAUTÉ.

3. Add lamb pieces, thyme, bay leaf and season with salt & pepper. Top with sliced potatoes. Brush the top with melted butter.

4. Close the lid with valve is in the seal position and move the slider to pressure. Cook on high for 18 minutes. Select Start/Stop to begin cooking. Select DELAYED RELEASE and set time for 10 mins. Select Start/Stop to begin cooking.

5. Move the slider to AIR FRY/HOB. Select AIR FRY, set the temperature to 190°C/375°F, and set the time to 10 minutes. Press START/STOP to begin cooking.

6. Open lid and let to rest for 5 minutes, then serve.

TOAD IN THE HOLE

 40 Minutes Serves 4

Ingredients:

- 450g sausages, slightly browned

Batter:
- 180g plain flour
- 340ml milk
- 2 tbsp butter
- 3 eggs
- ¼ tsp baking powder
- Pinch salt

Steps:

1. In a large bowl, add all batter ingredients. Whisk until combined and smooth.
2. Grease 23 x 23-cm baking dish. Put sausages in the dish, and pour the batter over sausages.
3. Add 350ml water to bottom of Ninja Foodi. Place bottom layer of Deluxe Reversible Rack in the lower position. Place the dish on top of rack, then place rack in the pot.
4. Close the lid with valve is in the seal position and move the slider to COMBI-STEAM. Select Steam & Bake set temperature to 190°C/375°F, and time to 30 minutes. Select Start/Stop to begin cooking. Serve.

PULLED BEEF

 30 Minutes Serves 8

Ingredients:

- 1 kg braising steak
- 2 garlic cloves, minced
- 125ml red wine vinegar
- 2 Tbsp tomato puree
- 50g brown sugar

- 500ml beef stock
- 1 tsp fennel seeds
- 1 bay leaf
- Salt & pepper to taste

Steps:

1. In a large bowl, add all ingredients except beef. Whisk until combined. Pour in Ninja Foodi pot. Add the beef, and cover with the marinade.
2. Close the lid with valve is in the seal position and move the slider to pressure. Cook on high for 60 minutes . Select DELAYED RELEASE and set time for 10 mins. Select Start/Stop to begin cooking.
3. Open lid, and shred beef with two forks in Ninja Foodi.
4. Move the slider to AIR FRY/HOB. Select SEAR/SAUTÉ and set the temperature to 5. Select START/STOP. Cook until liquid reduced to desired consistency.

PEPPER STEAK

🕐 **30 Minutes** 👤 **Serves 4**

Ingredients:

- 1 kg beef sirloin, cut into 5-cm pieces
- 3 garlic cloves, minced
- 3 tbsp oil
- 100ml beef stock
- 2 tbsp cornflour mixed with 2 tbsp water
- 1 large onion, chopped
- 2 large green bell peppers, roughly chopped
- 1 (375g) tin crushed or stewed tomatoes, undrained
- 3 tbsp soy sauce
- 1 tsp white sugar

Steps:

1. Add all ingredients (except bell pepper, corn flour and onion) into ninja foodi pot.
2. Close the lid with valve is in the seal position and move the slider to pressure. Cook on high for 30 minutes.Select DELAYED RELEASE and set time for 15 mins. Select Start/Stop to begin cooking.
3. Add in peppers and onions. Seal the Ninja foodi and cook on high pressure for 1 minutes, Select quick release.
4. Move the slider to AIR FRY/HOB. Select SEAR/SAUTÉ and set the temperature to 5. Select START/STOP, add cornflour mixture and stir until thickened.

SWISS STEAK

🕐 **40 Minutes** 👤 **Serves 6**

Ingredients:

- 4-6 braising steaks, tenderized
- 60g plain flour
- Salt & pepper to taste

Sauce

- 1 onion, diced
- 3 garlic cloves, minced
- 1 celery stalk, diced
- 1 carrot, diced
- 1 tsp dried oregano
- 1 Tbsp Worcestershire sauce
- 300g tin crushed tomatoes
- 240ml beef stock

Steps:

1. In a bowl, add flour, salt, and pepper. coat steaks in flour mixture.
2. Move the slider to AIR FRY/HOB. Select SEAR/SAUTÉ and set the temperature to HI-5. Select START/STOP, fry steaks in 1 tbsp oil until browned. Add remaining ingredients.
3. Close the lid with valve is in the seal position and move the slider to pressure. Cook on high for 30 minutes. Select DELAYED RELEASE and set time for 10 mins. Select Start/Stop to begin cooking.
4. Open lid, Serve steak with sauce on top.

SAUSAGE STEW

🕐 **25 Minutes** 👤 **Serves 4**

Ingredients:

- 4 sausage links, cut into 1-cm slices
- 1 medium onion, chopped
- 1 medium carrot, chopped
- 1 liter chicken stock
- 1 celery, chopped
- 1 medium potatoes, peeled & diced
- 1 clove garlic, minced
- Salt & pepper to taste
- ½ tsp. basil
- 1 tsp. oregano

Steps:

1. In your Ninja Foodi, add all ingredients. Mix until combined.
2. Close the lid with valve is in the seal position and move the slider to pressure. Cook on high for 5 minutes. Select DELAYED RELEASE and set time for 5 mins. Select Start/Stop to begin cooking.
3. Taste and add more salt, if desired.

BEEF AND CELERY STEW

🕐 **25 Minutes** 👤 **Serves 2**

Ingredients:

- 240ml beef stock
- 450g beef stew meat, cubed
- 100g celery, cubed
- 120ml tomato sauce
- 2 carrots, chopped
- 100g mushrooms, halved
- 1 medium onion, roughly chopped
- 1 tbsp olive oil
- Salt & pepper to taste
- 1 tbsp parsley, chopped

Steps:

1. In your Ninja Foodi, add all ingredients. Mix until combined.
2. Close the lid with valve is in the seal position and move the slider to pressure. Cook on high for 20 minutes. Select Start/Stop to begin cooking. Let pressure release naturally.
3. Divide stew into bowls and serve.

IRISH STEW

🕐 30 Minutes 👤 Serves 8

Ingredients:

- 1300g stew meat, cubed
- 60ml oil
- 1 large onion, chopped
- 1 liter beef stock
- 4 garlic cloves, minced
- 2 Tbsp tomato puree
- 1 Tbsp sugar
- 1 Tbsp soy sauce
- 2 tsp dried parsley
- ½ tsp dried thyme
- 2 bay leaves
- 450g potatoes, cubed
- 3 carrots peeled and cut into 2.5cm pieces

Steps:

1. Move the slider to AIR FRY/HOB. Select SEAR/SAUTÉ and set the temperature to 5. Select START/STOP, add oil and cook meat until browned on all sides. Add all remaining ingredients (except carrots and potatoes).
2. Close the lid with valve is in the seal position and move the slider to pressure. Cook on high for 30 minutes. Use the arrows to select PRESSURE RELEASE and select QUICK RELEASE. Select Start/Stop to begin cooking.
3. Open lid, add potatoes and carrots. Close lid and cook on high pressure for 4 minutes. Use the arrows to select PRESSURE RELEASE and select QUICK RELEASE.
4. Serve warm with bread.

BEEF AND BARLEY SOUP

Ingredients:

🕐 40 Minutes 👤 Serves 6

- 450g braising steak
- 100g barley
- 2 tbsp olive oil
- 2 carrots sliced
- 2 stalks celery sliced
- 1 onion chopped
- 2 potatoes peeled & cubed
- 1 tbsp worcestershire sauce
- 2 cloves garlic minced
- 1 tsp oregano
- 1 tsp basil
- ¼ tsp thyme
- 1 Tbsp parsley
- 1 liter beef stock
- 1 Tbsp white sugar
- 1 (800g) tin crushed tomatoes
- oil
- Salt & pepper to taste

Steps:

1. Move the slider to AIR FRY/HOB. Select SEAR/SAUTÉ and set the temperature to 5. Select START/STOP, add oil and cook meat until browned on all sides. Add all remaining ingredients and stir.
2. Close the lid with valve is in the seal position and move the slider to pressure. Cook on high for 15 minutes. Select DELAYED RELEASE and set time for 15 mins. Select Start/Stop to begin cooking.
3. Serve with Buttermilk Biscuits.

SWEDE BEEF STEW

🕐 45 Minutes 👤 Serves 4

Ingredients:

- 1¼ kg braising steak, cubed
- 3 swedes, peeled and cubed
- 1 potato, peeled and cubed
- 1 carrot, sliced
- 1 turnip, peeled and cubed

- 2 cloves garlic, peeled and minced
- 1 onion, cut into wedges
- 600ml beef stock
- 2 tbsp tomato puree
- 1 tbsp Worcestershire sauce
- Salt & pepper to taste

Steps:

1. Move the slider to AIR FRY/HOB. Select SEAR/SAUTÉ and set the temperature to HI-5. Select START/STOP, add oil and cook meat until browned on all sides. Add all remaining ingredients and stir.
2. Close the lid with valve is in the seal position and move the slider to pressure. Cook on high for 30 minutes. Select DELAYED RELEASE and set time for 15 mins. Select Start/Stop to begin cooking.
3. Serve with biscuits.

MEXICAN BEEF STEW

🕐 45 Minutes 👤 Serves 6

Ingredients:

- 1 kg braising steak, cubed
- 1 tin (800g) diced tomatoes, undrained
- 1 large onions, chopped
- 1 tsp chili powder
- 2 tbsp taco seasoning mix

- 1 tin (450g) black beans, drained & rinsed
- 1 tin (300g) kernel corn, drained
- 1 green chilli, chopped
- Salt & pepper to taste

Steps:

1. Move the slider to AIR FRY/HOB. Select SEAR/SAUTÉ and set the temperature to HI-5. Select START/STOP, add oil and cook meat until browned on all sides. Add all remaining ingredients and stir.
2. Close the lid with valve is in the seal position and move the slider to pressure. Cook on high for 35 minutes. Select DELAYED RELEASE and set time for 13 mins. Select Start/Stop to begin cooking.
3. Serve topped with cheese and scallion.

SCOTTISH STOVIES

🕐 45 Minutes 👤 Serves 3

Ingredients:

- 1 kg potatoes, peeled & thickly chopped
- 450g braising steak, cubed
- 600ml beef stock
- 2 medium carrots, peeled & diced
- 1 onion, peeled & chopped
- Salt & pepper to taste
- 4 tbsp flour
- oil for frying

Steps:

1. In a large bowl, add flour and season with salt & pepper. Add meat and mix until coated with flour.
2. Move the slider to AIR FRY/HOB. Select SEAR/SAUTÉ and set the temperature to HI-5. Select START/STOP, add oil and cook meat until browned on all sides. Add all remaining ingredients and stir.
3. Close the lid with valve is in the seal position and move the slider to pressure. Cook on high for 40 minutes. Select DELAYED RELEASE and set time for 10 mins. Select Start/Stop to begin cooking.
4. Open lid, divide into bowls and serve.

SCOTCH BROTH

🕐 45 Minutes 👤 Serves 4

Ingredients:

- 1 kg lamb shanks, cut into small cubes
- 120g dried peas
- 100g Pearl barley
- 2 liter beef sock
- 250g carrots, diced
- 250g turnip, diced
- 1 large onion, diced
- salt & pepper to taste

Steps:

1. Move the slider to AIR FRY/HOB. Select SEAR/SAUTÉ and set the temperature to HI-5. Select START/STOP, add oil and cook meat until browned on all sides. Add all remaining ingredients and stir.
2. Close the lid with valve is in the seal position and move the slider to pressure. Cook on high for 20 minutes. Select DELAYED RELEASE and set time for 10 mins. Select Start/Stop to begin cooking.
3. Adjust seasoning if desired, stir and serve.

SAUSAGE & BUTTER BEAN CASSEROLE

 30 Minutes   Serves 5

Ingredients:

- ½ tbsp oil
- 350g sausages
- 1 onion, finely chopped
- 1 celery stick, finely chopped
- 1 large garlic clove, minced
- ½ tbsp smoked paprika
- 6 thyme sprigs
- 750ml chicken stock
- 250g butter beans, soaked for 8 hours & drained
- 1 (375g) tin chopped tomatoes
- ½ tbsp caster sugar
- ½ tbsp vinegar
- Salt & pepper to taste

Steps:

1. Move the slider to AIR FRY/HOB. Select SEAR/SAUTÉ and set the temperature to HI-5. Select START/STOP to preheat Ninja foodi for 5 minutes, add little oil and brown the sausages for 5 minutes or so until well browned. Remove and set aside.

2. Add onion and celery, season with salt and cook until soft. Add stock along with the remaining ingredients (except sausage). Stirring and scrapping the bottom of the pot.

3. Close the lid with valve is in the seal position and move the slider to pressure. Cook on high for 20 minutes. Select DELAYED RELEASE and set time for 10 mins. Select Start/Stop to begin cooking.

4. Open lid, add sausage. Close lid, Cook on high for 3 minutes. Select Start/Stop to begin cooking. Then Use the arrows to select PRESSURE RELEASE and select QUICK RELEASE.

5. Open lid, adjust seasoning and serve.

BANGERS AND MASH

🕐 **40 Minutes** 👤 **Serves 4**

Ingredients:

- 1 kg potatoes, peeled and cut into 2.5cm cubes
- 240ml water
- 1 kg sausages
- 60g unsalted butter + 2 tbsp
- 4 tbsp double cream
- 2 onions, cut into slices
- 300ml beef stock
- 2 tsp Worcestershire sauce
- 2 tbsp balsamic vinegar
- 2 tbsp cornflour mixed with 2 tbsp water
- Salt & pepper to taste

Steps:

1. In your Ninja Foodi, add potatoes and water. Add sausage on top in a single layer.
2. Close the lid with valve is in the seal position and move the slider to pressure. Cook on high for 10 minutes. Use the arrows to select PRESSURE RELEASE and select QUICK RELEASE. Select Start/Stop to begin cooking.
3. Move slider to Air Fry/HOB to unlock the lid, then carefully open it. Transfer sausage to a plate and transfer potatoes into a bowl.
4. Add the double cream, 60g butter, salt & pepper to the potatoes. Use a potato masher to mash the potatoes to the desired consistency. (add more salt and double cream if necessary).
5. Move the slider to AIR FRY/HOB. Select SEAR/SAUTÉ and set the temperature to HI-5. Select START/STOP to preheat Ninja foodi for 5 minutes.
6. Add 2 tbsp butter Ninja Foodi pot. Then add onions. Sauté until onions softened and brown, for 4 minutes. Pour in the Worcestershire sauce and balsamic vinegar and stir.
7. Pour stock along with cornflour/water mixture. Whisk until it begins to thicken. Season with salt and pepper.
8. Plate the mashed potatoes, sausages, and gravy. Serve immediately.

BEEF GOULASH

🕐 1 ½ Hours 👤 Serves 6

Ingredients:

- 1 kg beef brisket or flank steak cut into large chunks
- 1 tbsp paprika
- 2 tbsp plain flour
- 4 tbsp oil
- 2 large onions, chopped
- 2 tbsp tomato puree
- 2 garlic cloves crushed
- 1 bay leaf
- 125ml beef stock
- 375ml tin crushed tomato
- 3 red peppers, chopped
- 2 tbsp cider vinegar
- Salt & pepper to taste
- 2 tbsp cornflour mixed with 2 tbsp water

Steps:

1. In a large ziplock bag, add flour, paprika, salt & pepper. Add meat, close bag and shake to coat.
2. Move the slider to AIR FRY/HOB. Select SEAR/SAUTÉ and set the temperature to HI-5. Select START/STOP to preheat Ninja foodi for 5 minutes.
3. Add oil and brown the beef (in batches) until browned on all sides. Transfer beef to a plate.
4. Add onion, season with salt and Sauté until soft.
5. Add browned beef to Ninja Foodi pot along with the remaining ingredients. Stir & scrape the bottom of the pot to loosen any browned bits of beef.
6. Close the lid with valve is in the seal position and move the slider to pressure. Cook on high for 15 minutes, let the pressure release naturally. Select Start/Stop to begin cooking.
7. Move slider to Air Fry/HOB to unlock the lid, then carefully open it.
8. Pour cornflour/water mixture into the pot. Whisk until it begins to thicken. Season with salt and pepper. Serve.

LEMON GARLIC ROAST CHICKEN

Ingredients:

- 2 kg whole chicken , patted dry
- 1 tsp dried thyme
- ½ tsp dried parsley
- ½ tsp dried oregano
- 4 tbsp melted butter
- 3 garlic cloves , minced
- 1 large lemon , zest & juice
- salt & pepper

Steps:

1. In a large bowl, add thyme, parsley, oregano, butter, garlic, salt & pepper.
2. Use a spoon to loosen chicken skin. Spoon ¾ of spices mixture under skin. Use hands to spread remaining spices over chicken skin. Add lemon inside the chicken.
3. Add 350ml water to bottom of Ninja Foodi. Add Foodi Cook & Crisp basket in, add chicken in the basket.
4. Close lid and cook on high pressure for 22 mins. Select DELAYED RELEASE and set time for 5 mins. Select Start/Stop to begin cooking.
5. Move slider to Air Fry/HOB to unlock the lid, then carefully open it.
6. Brush the chicken with melted butter and sprinkle with salt & pepper.
7. Close the lid with valve is in the seal position and move the slider to COMBI-STEAM. Select Steam & Crisp set temperature to 190°C/375°F, and time to 8 minutes. Select Start/Stop to begin cooking.
8. Remove chicken from Ninja Foodi and allow it to rest for 10 minutes before slicing.

LEMON PEPPER CHICKEN

Ingredients:

- 600g boneless skinless chicken thighs
- 1 tbsp oil
- 1 lemon juice & zest
- 1½ tsp garlic powder
- Salt & pepper to taste

Lemon pepper butter sauce
- 2 tbsp Butter (melted)
- 1 large lemon , zest & juice
- ½ tsp ground black pepper
- Salt to taste

Steps:

1. Pat chicken dry with paper towel, then place in a bowl, add oil, lemon juice, zest, salt, pepper and garlic powder. mix till coated with marinade, cover and marinade for 30 mins in the refrigerator.
2. Place marinated chicken thighs in Foodi Cook & Crisp basket. Place basket in Ninja Foodi.
3. Close the lid and move the slider to AIR FRY/HOB. Select AIR FRY, set the temperature to 190°C/375°F, and set the time to 18 minutes. Press START/STOP to begin cooking. Flip halfway through cooking time.
4. Mix all the lemon pepper butter sauce. Brush sauce all over chicken and serve.

CHICKEN POT PIE

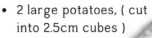 🕐 **40 Minutes**   👤 **Serves 6**

Ingredients:

Pie Crust
- 300g plain flour
- 1 tsp salt
- 270g unsalted butter, (cut into small cubes)
- 5 to 6 tbsp iced water

Pie Filling
- 75g plus 1 tbsp unsalted butter, divided
- 1 onion, (diced)
- 1 celery stalk, (chopped)
- 125ml chicken stock
- 2 large boneless skinless chicken breasts, (cut into bite-size pieces)

- 2 large potatoes, (cut into 2.5cm cubes)
- ¼ tsp dried thyme
- 140g frozen peas and carrots
- 50g plain flour
- 125ml milk, plus more as needed
- Salt & pepper to taste

Steps:

1. In a large mixing bowl, add flour & salt. Mix until combined. Add the butter into the flour mixture, Mash with fork until resembles very coarse meal. Gradually add water until dough just sticks together into ball.

2. Move the slider to AIR FRY/HOB. Select SEAR/SAUTÉ and set the temperature to HI-5. Select START/STOP to preheat Ninja foodi for 5 minutes.

3. Add the 1 tbsp butter to Ninja. Add onion, celery and sauté for 3 minutes, until tender. Add chicken stock, chicken, potatoes, thyme, and season with salt & pepper.

4. Close the lid with valve is in the seal position and move the slider to pressure. Cook on high for 3 minutes. Select Start/Stop to begin cooking. Use the arrows to select PRESSURE RELEASE and select QUICK RELEASE. Select Start/Stop to begin cooking.

5. Move slider to Air Fry/HOB to unlock the lid, then carefully open it.

6. Add the peas and carrots. Whisk in remaining butter and flour. Cook for 3 minutes, until bubbly. Gradually add milk, stirring for 2 more minutes, until the sauce is thick and creamy.

7. Grease a deep-dish pie. Transfer the pie crust into floured surface and roll it into a circle that's at least 2.5cm larger than the baking dish.

8. Pour chicken mixture into the pie dish. Top with the pie crust (poke some holes in the crust top).

9. Add 250ml water to bottom of Ninja Foodi. Place bottom layer of Deluxe Reversible Rack in the lower position. Place the pie dish on top of rack, then place rack in the ninja pot.

10. Close the lid with valve is in the seal position and move the slider to COMBI-STEAM. Select Steam & Bake set temperature to 190°C/375°F, and time to 15 minutes. Select Start/Stop to begin cooking.

CHICKEN PASTIES

 40 Minutes  Serves 6-8

Ingredients:

Pasties
- 500g plain flour
- 250g cold butter
- 1 egg , beaten for brushing
- 150ml water

Filling
- 1 swede, diced
- 1 onion, , diced
- 1 medium carrots, diced
- 1 celery stalk, diced
- 2 boneless skinless chicken breasts, (cut into 1-cm pieces)

- 60g plain flour
- 1 tsp mustard seeds
- 120g grated cheddar cheese
- 60ml melted butter
- Salt & pepper to taste

Steps:

1. In a large bowl, add all filling ingredients, mix, then set aside.
2. In a large mixing bowl, add flour & salt. Mix until combined. Add the butter into the flour mixture, Mash with fork until resembles very coarse meal. Gradually add water until dough just sticks together into ball. Do not over mix.
3. Divide dough into 8 equal balls. Transfer into a floured, then roll out each pastry to 20-cm circle. Repeat until you have 8 circles.
4. Fill each pastie with even amount of filling on one side of each pastry circle and brush edges with beaten egg. Fold top half of the pasty down over the filling, pressing down to seal with your thumb to press down and seal around the edges. Brush pasties tops with egg.
5. Place pasties in Foodi Cook & Crisp basket. Place basket in Ninja Foodi.
6. Close the lid and move the slider to AIR FRY/HOB. Select AIR FRY, set the temperature to 190°C/375°F, and set the time to 35 minutes. Press START/STOP to begin cooking. Flip halfway through cooking time. Check pasties if they` re not done cook for more 5-8 Minutes.
7. Serve.

CHICKEN TIKKA MASALA

🕐 30 Minutes 👤 Serves 8

Ingredients:

- 8 boneless, skinless chicken thighs, each cut into 3 chunks
- 2 tbsp oil
- 1 large onion, chopped
- 2 garlic cloves, minced
- 2 tsp ginge, finely grated
- 3 tbsp tikka curry paste

- 500ml crushed tomatoes
- 1 tbsp vinegar
- 1 tbsp light brown soft sugar
- 1 cinnamon stick
- 5 cardamom pods
- 100ml double cream
- Salt & pepper to taste

Steps:

1. Move the slider to AIR FRY/HOB. Select SEAR/SAUTÉ and set the temperature to HI-5. Select START/STOP to preheat Ninja foodi for 5 minutes. Add onions and sauté until soft. Add chicken pieces and cook until browned on all sides. Add all ingredients into Ninja pot except double cream. Stir.

2. Close the lid with valve is in seal position and move slider to pressure. Cook on high for 8 minutes. Use the arrows to select PRESSURE RELEASE and select QUICK RELEASE. Select Start/Stop to begin cooking.

3. Move slider to AIR FRY/HOB. Select SEAR/SAUTÉ and set to medium heat. Add cream and adjust seasoning, stir until slightly thickens. serve with rice.

CHICKEN BALTI

🕐 45 Minutes 👤 Serves 4

Ingredients:

- 2 tbsp oil
- 500g skinless, boneless chicken thighs
- 1 onion, chopped
- 1 red bell pepper, chopped
- 2 green chillies, chopped
- 2 tsp ground cumin
- 2 tsp ground coriander
- 1 tsp turmeric

- 1 tsp smoked paprika
- 1 tsp garam masala
- 3 tsp grated ginger
- 4 cloves garlic, minced
- 2 tbs tomato puree
- 375g tin crushed tomatoes
- 100 ml water
- salt & pepper to taste

Steps:

1. Move the slider to AIR FRY/HOB. Select SEAR/SAUTÉ and set the temperature to HI-5. Select START/STOP to preheat Ninja foodi for 5 minutes. Add onions and sauté until soft. Add chicken pieces and cook until browned on all sides. Add all ingredients into Ninja pot. Stir.

2. Close the lid with valve is in the seal position and move the slider to pressure. Cook on high for 7 minutes. Let the pressure release naturally. Select Start/Stop to begin cooking.

3. Adjust seasonings and serve.

ORANGE CHICKEN

🕐 40 Minutes 👤 Serves 6

Ingredients:

- 1 tbsp oil
- 4 boneless, skinless chicken breasts cut into 2.5cm cubes
- 230g orange marmalade
- 240ml unsweetened orange juice
- 120ml soy sauce

- 60g cornflour, divided
- 120ml chicken stock
- 50ml honey
- 2 tbsp vinegar
- 2 tsp minced garlic
- 2 tsp minced ginger
- 1 pinch red pepper flakes
- salt & pepper to taste

Steps:

1. In a mixing bowl, add 30g cornflour salt & pepper. Add chicken and mix to coat.
2. Move the slider to AIR FRY/HOB. Select SEAR/SAUTÉ and set the temperature to HI-5. Select START/STOP to preheat for 5 minutes. Add oil, brown chicken in batches, until golden.
3. In a bowl, add marmalade, juice, soy sauce, stock, honey, vinegar, garlic, ginger and red pepper flakes. Whisk until combined. Pour over chicken in Ninja Foodi. Stir & scrape bottom of pot to loosen any browned bits of chicken.
4. Close the lid with valve is in the seal position and move the slider to pressure. Cook on high for 7 minutes. Select DELAYED RELEASE and set time for 10 mins. Select Start/Stop to begin cooking.
5. Move slider to Air Fry/HOB to unlock the lid, then carefully open it.
6. Mix remaining Cornflour with 2 tbsp. of water. Stir half of Cornflour mixture into the sauce and cook, stirring, until thickened. Keep adding Cornflour mixture until thickens as desired.

CHICKEN PICCATA

⏱ **30 Minutes** 👤 **Serves 4**

Ingredients:

- 700g chicken breasts, skinless & boneless
- 3 tablespoons oil
- 30g plain flour
- 50g grated Old Winchester/Parmesan
- 1 teaspoon dried oregano
- 1 teaspoon dried basil
- 3 tablespoons butter
- 300ml chicken stock
- 50g chopped green olives or capers
- 60ml fresh lemon juice
- 2 tablespoons cornflour mixed with 4 tbsp water
- Salt & pepper to taste

Steps:

1. Butterfly chicken breasts, and then cut them through. Pound with a tenderizer until all even in thickness. Season with salt & pepper.
2. In a bowl add flour, oregano, basil, and grated cheese. Mix and add chicken pieces in flour/cheese mixture, until both sides coated.
3. Move the slider to AIR FRY/HOB. Select SEAR/SAUTÉ and set the temperature to HI-5. Select START/STOP to preheat for 5 minutes. Add oil, brown chicken in batches, until golden.
4. Add chicken stock, stir & scrape bottom of pot to loosen any browned bits of chicken. Add all remaining ingredients to the pot except (cornflour/water mixture).
5. Close the lid with valve is in the seal position and move the slider to pressure. Cook on high for 4 minutes. Select DELAYED RELEASE and set time for 5 mins. Select Start/Stop to begin cooking.
6. Move slider to Air Fry/HOB to unlock the lid, then carefully open it.
7. Open lid, remove chicken from pot and set aside.
8. Move the slider to AIR FRY/HOB. Select SEAR/SAUTÉ and set the temperature to 4. Select START/STOP, add cornflour/water mixture. Stir and cook for until thickened, then spoon over chicken. Serve.

HUNTERS CHICKEN

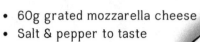 🕐 35 Minutes 👤 Serves 4

Ingredients:

- 4 chicken breasts
- 8 strips streaky beef bacon
- 240ml BBQ sauce
- 60g grated cheddar cheese
- 60g grated mozzarella cheese
- Salt & pepper to taste

Steps:

1. Wrap each chicken breast in two strips of bacon.
2. Transfer chicken to a baking dish that will fit in your ninja. Place bottom layer of Deluxe Reversible Rack in the lower position. Place the baking dish on top of rack, then place rack in the ninja.
3. Close the and move the slider to AIR FRY/HOB. Select AIR FRY and set temperature to 190° C/375° F. Set time for 25 minutes. Press START/STOP to begin cooking.
4. Remove the baking dish from the Ninja Foodi. Spoon the BBQ sauce on chicken, then sprinkle with cheese.
5. Close the and move the slider to AIR FRY/HOB. Select AIR FRY and set temperature to 190° C/375° F. Set time for 5 minutes. Press START/STOP to begin cooking.
6. Open lid, serve with mash and vegetables.

BUTTERMILK CHICKEN

 🕐 1 Hour 👤 Serves 4

Ingredients:

- 3 garlic cloves, minced
- 300ml buttermilk
- 2 tsp dried rosemary
- 1 tbsp brown sugar
- 8 chicken drumsticks
- Salt & pepper to taste

Steps:

1. In a large bowl, add all ingredients. Cover the bowl and leave in the fridge for at least 8 hours.
2. Take chicken out of marinade, shake off excess buttermilk and garlic.
3. Add Foodi Cook & Crisp basket in, add chicken drumsticks in single layer inside of Ninja Foodi basket.
4. Close the lid with valve is in the seal position and move the slider to COMBI-STEAM. Select Steam & Crisp set temperature to 180°C/360°F, and time to 35-40 minutes. Select Start/Stop to begin cooking. (Flip chicken halfway through cooking time)
5. Serve with roasted potatoes.

CHICKEN SHAWARMA

🕐 **15 Minutes** 👤 **Serves 4**

Ingredients:

- 6 large skinless, boneless chicken breast, cut half lengthwise

Marinade:
- 1 tbs oil
- 1 lemon juice
- 1 tsp ground cumin
- 1 tsp smoked paprika
- 1 tsp ground coriander
- ½ tsp cinnamon
- ¼ tsp dried chilli flakes
- Salt & pepper to taste

Steps:

1. In a bowl, add marinade ingredients, mix. Place chicken in a ziplock bag and add marinade. Coat chicken with marinade. Place in refrigerator for 6 hours or overnight.

2. Add chicken strips to top layer of greased Deluxe Reversible Rack. Place rack into Ninja.

3. Close the and move the slider to AIR FRY/HOB. Select AIR FRY and set temperature to 195° C/380° F. Set time for 10 minutes. Press START/STOP to begin cooking. (Remove rack half way through cook time and flip chicken).

4. Open lid, and slice the chicken. Serve with flat bread, over salad or rice.

CORNISH HEN

🕐 **40 Minutes** 👤 **Serves 4**

Ingredients:

- 2 cornish hens, (700g each)
- 2 tbsp olive oil
- 1 ½ tsp Italian seasoning
- 1 tsp garlic powder
- 1 tsp smoked paprika
- 1 tbsp lemon juice
- Salt & pepper to taste

Steps:

1. Pat dry hens with paper towels. Set aside.

2. In a medium bowl, mix all of the seasonings. Brush the hens with olive oil and then coat with the seasonings.

3. Put the hens, breast side down to top layer of greased Deluxe Reversible Rack. Place rack into Ninja.

4. Close the and move the slider to AIR FRY/HOB. Select AIR FRY and set temperature to 180° C/350° F. Set time for 45 minutes. Press START/STOP to begin cooking. (Remove rack half way through cook time and flip chicken.)

5. Open lid, remove from Ninja, let the hen rest for 11 minutes before carving.

CHICKEN PHAAL

🕐 30 Minutes 👤 Serves 4

Ingredients:

- 450g chicken breasts, chopped
- 1 tbsp oil
- 3 hot peppers, seeded & chopped
- 1 onion, chopped
- 4 cloves garlic, minced
- 1 tbsp grated fresh ginger
- 1 tbsp curry powder
- 1 tsp paprika
- 1 tsp cardamom powder
- 1 tsp turmeric
- 1 tsp cumin
- 2 tbsp tomato puree
- 1 (375g) tin crushed tomatoes
- 240ml chicken stock
- Salt & pepper to taste

Steps:

1. Move the slider to AIR FRY/HOB. Select SEAR/SAUTÉ and set the temperature to HI-5. Select START/STOP to preheat Ninja foodi for 5 minutes, add oil, hot peppers and onion. Saute for 5 minutes, until softened. Add chicken and cook, until golden.

2. Add all remaining ingredients to the ninja pot, stirring and scrapping the bottom of the pot to loose any stuck pieces.

3. Close the lid with valve is in the seal position and move the slider to pressure. Cook on high for 6 mins. Use the arrows to select PRESSURE RELEASE and select QUICK RELEASE. Select Start/Stop to begin cooking.

4. Move slider to Air Fry/HOB to unlock the lid, then carefully open it.

5. Open lid, Serve over white rice.

HONEY GARLIC CHICKEN

🕐 30 Minutes 👤 Serves 4

Ingredients:

- 8 chicken thigh cutlets, skin on
- **Honey garlic sauce:**
- 60ml honey
- 60ml soy sauce
- 60ml tomato sauce
- 3 garlic cloves, minced
- 60ml chicken stock
- Salt & pepper to taste

Steps:

1. Move the slider to AIR FRY/HOB. Select SEAR/SAUTÉ and set the temperature to HI-5. Select START/STOP, add oil. Once hot, add chicken skin side down first and cook, until golden brown. Remove from ninja foodi and set aside.

2. In a bowl, mix all sauce ingredients and mix. Pour into ninja foodi and stir, scrapping the bottom of pot to make sure there is no stuck pieces. Add back the chicken.

3. Close the lid with valve is in the seal position and move the slider to pressure. Cook on high for 10 mins. Use the arrows to select PRESSURE RELEASE and select QUICK RELEASE.

4. Open lid, serve the chicken with honey garlic sauce.

CHEESE STUFFED CHICKEN BREAST

🕐 20 Minutes 👤 Serves 4

Ingredients:

- 2 medium sized chicken breasts
- 120g gouda slices
- 200 Salami
- 1 large egg, (beaten)
- 100g bread crumbs
- 1 tsp Italian Seasoning
- 1 tbsp butter, (melted)
- salt & pepper to taste

Steps:

1. Cut chicken breasts in half horizontally through the middle. With meat tenderizer pound the chicken breasts to about ½cm thin. Season with salt & pepper.

2. Put 3 gouda slices, and 4 salami slices on each chicken breast. Roll chicken and secure with, toothpicks.

3. In a dish, mix breadcrumbs & Italian seasoning. Roll chicken in beaten egg, coat with breadcrumbs.

4. Add Foodi Cook & Crisp basket in, add chicken in single layer inside of the basket, brush with butter.

5. Close the and move the slider to AIR FRY/HOB. Select AIR FRY and set temperature to 190° C/375° F. Set time for 20 minutes. Press START/STOP to begin cooking. (Remove rack half way through cook time and flip chicken.)

6. Remove from the basket and serve.

CHICKPEA CHICKEN CURRY

🕐 **40 Minutes**   👤 **Serves 6**

Ingredients:

- 1 tbsp oil
- 1kg chicken thighs, halved
- 375g tin chickpeas, rinsed & drained
- 1 onion, chopped
- 2 garlic cloves, minced
- 2 tsp fresh grated ginger
- 60g curry paste
- 375g tin crushed tomatoes
- 100ml chicken stock
- 120g yogurt
- Salt & pepper to taste

Steps:

1. Move the slider to AIR FRY/HOB. Select SEAR/SAUTÉ and set the temperature to HI-5. Select START/STOP, add oil. Once hot, add chicken skin side down first and cook, until golden brown. Remove from ninja foodi and set aside. Add all remaining ingredients (except yogurt and chickpeas).

2. Close the lid with valve is in the seal position and move the slider to pressure. Cook on high for 15 mins. Use the arrows to select PRESSURE RELEASE and select QUICK RELEASE. Select Start/Stop to begin cooking.

3. Move slider to Air Fry/HOB to unlock the lid, then carefully open it. add yogurt and chickpeas. Stir.

4. Close the lid with valve is in the seal position and move the slider to pressure. Cook on high for 3 mins. Use the arrows to select PRESSURE RELEASE and select QUICK RELEASE. Select Start/Stop to begin cooking. Move slider to Air Fry/HOB to unlock the lid, then carefully open it.

5. Serve with rice, salad or bread.

CHICKEN STEW & DUMPLINGS

⏱ 50 Minutes 👤 Serves 6

Ingredients:

- 1 litre chicken stock
- 1 ½ kg chicken breasts, cut into bite size pieces
- 2 teaspoons oil
- 1 large onion, chopped
- 250g celeriac/potatoes, chopped
- 2 celery stalks, trimmed & chopped
- 3 tbsp tomato puree
- 3 carrots, peeled and sliced
- 1 teaspoon dried thyme
- 40g plain flour
- Salt & pepper to taste

For the dumbling
- 250g self raising flour
- ¾ teaspoon salt
- 2 tablespoons butter, melted
- 125g cold butter, grated
- water

Steps:

1. In a bowl, add flour, butter, and salt. Mix until mixture resembles large crumbs. Gradually drizzle in water, until mixture starts to form a ball and holds together. Don't over mix. Divide into 12 pieces and roll into balls.

2. Move the slider to AIR FRY/HOB. Select SEAR/SAUTÉ and set the temperature to HI-5. Select START/STOP, add oil. Once hot, add chicken and cook, until golden brown. Add onions, garlic, celery and carrots. Sauté until fragrant.

3. Add all ingredients to the Ninja Foodi.

4. Close the lid with valve is in the seal position and move the slider to pressure. Cook on high for 12 mins. Select DELAYED RELEASE and set time for 5 mins. Select Start/Stop to begin cooking.

5. In a bowl, add flour, butter, and salt. Mix until mixture resembles large crumbs. Gradually drizzle in water, until mixture starts to form a ball and holds together. Don't over mix. Divide into 10 pieces and roll into balls.

6. Open lid, place the balls on top of stew.

7. Close the lid and move the slider to AIR FRY/HOB. Select AIR FRY, set the temperature to 190°C/375°F, and set the time to 25 minutes. Press START/STOP to begin cooking.

8. Serve hot.

HUNTER'S CHICKEN STEW

🕐 35 Minutes 👤 Serves 6

Ingredients:

- 1kg chicken thighs, drumsticks skin in, bone in
- 2 bell peppers, sliced
- 225g mushroom, chopped
- 1 onion, chopped
- 2 garlic cloves, minced
- 800g tin crushed tomatoes
- 120ml chicken stock
- 1 tsp. dried oregano
- ¼ tsp. red pepper flakes
- 50g olives, pitted
- Salt & pepper to taste

Steps:

1. Move the slider to AIR FRY/HOB. Select SEAR/SAUTÉ and set the temperature to HI-5. Select START/STOP to preheat Ninja foodi for 5 minutes, add oil, chicken and cook, until golden.
2. Add all remaining ingredients, stir and scrape the bottom of the pot.
3. Close the lid with valve is in the seal position and move the slider to pressure. Cook on high for 12 mins. Use the arrows to select PRESSURE RELEASE and select QUICK RELEASE. Select Start/Stop to begin cooking.
4. Move slider to Air Fry/HOB to unlock the lid, then carefully open it.
5. Open lid, then stir, taste and add a little salt and pepper if necessary and serve salad.

CHICKEN AND MUSHROOMS

🕐 25 Minutes 👤 Serves 6

Ingredients:

- 1 kg chicken breasts, cut into cubes
- 1 onion, diced
- 2 garlic cloves, minced
- 450g mushrooms, sliced
- 2 tsp Dijon mustard
- 1 tsp dried oregano
- 350ml chicken stock
- 125ml double cream
- 3 Tbsp cornflour mixed with 3 Tbsp water
- Salt & pepper to taste

Steps:

1. Move the slider to AIR FRY/HOB. Select SEAR/SAUTÉ and set the temperature to HI-5. Select START/STOP to preheat Ninja foodi for 5 minutes, add oil, chicken and cook, until golden. Remove chicken from ninja and set aside.

2. Add mushrooms and saute until golden. Add chicken back to the Ninja pot. Cancel saute.

3. Add all remaining ingredients except (cream and cornflour/water mixture) . Mix scrapping the bottom of the pot.

4. Close the lid with valve is in the seal position and move the slider to pressure. Cook on high for 12 mins. Use the arrows to select PRESSURE RELEASE and select QUICK RELEASE. Select Start/Stop to begin cooking.

5. Move slider to Air Fry/HOB to unlock the lid, then carefully open it.

6. Open lid, move the slider to AIR FRY/HOB. Select SEAR/SAUTÉ and set the temperature to 3. Select START/STOP. Stir cornflour/water mixture and the cream into liquid in Ninja Foodi. Stir until the mushroom sauce thickens. Adjust seasoning.

7. Serve with rice or pasta.

MULLIGATAWNY SOUP

Ingredients:

⏱ 30 Minutes 👤 Serves 6

- 60ml oil
- 8 garlic cloves, minced
- 2 carrots, peeled & chopped
- 2 celery stalks, sliced
- 1 large apple, peeled & and chopped
- 450g boneless, skinless chicken thighs, cut to bite-size chunks
- 150g red lentils

- 2 tbsp tomato puree
- 2 tbsp grated ginger
- 2 tsp mustard seeds
- 1 tsp ground turmeric
- 1 tsp curry powder
- ½tsp cumin seeds
- 1 liter chicken stock
- 120ml coconut cream
- Juice of 1 lime
- Salt & pepper to taste

Steps:

1. Move the slider to AIR FRY/HOB. Select SEAR/SAUTÉ and set the temperature to HI-5. Select START/STOP to preheat Ninja foodi for 5 minutes, add oil, carrot and onion. Saute for 5 minutes, until softened. Add chicken and cook, until golden.
2. Add the garlic, and ginger and cook for 30 seconds. Add spices. Cook for 1 minute. add all remaining ingredients except (coconut cream).
3. Close the lid with valve is in the seal position and move the slider to pressure. Cook on high for 10 mins. Use arrows to select PRESSURE RELEASE, select QUICK RELEASE. Select Start/Stop to begin cooking.
4. Open lid, Add coconut cream. Stir and serve.

CHICKEN NOODLE SOUP

⏱ 30 Minutes 👤 Serves 6

Ingredients:

- 700g boneless, skinless chicken breasts
- 2 liter chicken stock
- 4 garlic cloves , minced
- 1 onion, diced
- 2 carrots, shredded

- 3 stalks celery, diced
- ½ tsp dried thyme
- ½ tsp dried rosemary
- 2 bay leaves
- 225g spaghetti, broken into thirds
- Salt & pepper to taste

Steps:

1. Move the slider to AIR FRY/HOB. Select SEAR/SAUTÉ and set the temperature to HI-5. Select START/STOP to preheat Ninja foodi for 5 minutes, add oil, carrot, celery and onion. Saute for 5 minutes, until softened. Add chicken, cook until golden. Add all remaining ingredients except spaghetti.
2. Close the lid with valve is in the seal position and move slider to pressure. Cook on high for 7 mins. Select DELAYED RELEASE and set time for 10 mins. Select Start/Stop to begin cooking.
3. Open lid, remove chicken and shred with two forks. Move the slider to AIR FRY/HOB. Select SEAR/SAUTÉ and add spaghetti. Let simmer for 5 mins. Add back shredded chicken.
4. Serve with bread slices.

CHICKEN PARMESAN

🕐 20 Minutes 👤 Serves 4

Ingredients:

- 4 chicken breasts halves, skinless and boneless
- 60g plain flour
- 2 eggs
- 150g breadcrumbs
- 1 tsp basil, chopped
- 500g grated parmesan

Topping:
- 500g marinara sauce
- 200g cheddar cheese, shredded
- 50g parmesan, shredded
- Salt & pepper to taste

Steps:

1. Pound the chicken breasts into thinner pieces that are the same thickness.
2. In a bowl, add flour, salt, and pepper. In another bowl, beat eggs. In a third bowl, mix together the breadcrumbs, basil, and Parmesan.
3. Coat chicken in flour mixture, then in egg and finally cover in breadcrumbs until coated. Repeat for all chicken breasts.
4. Add 240ml water to Ninja Foodi pot. Add Foodi Cook & Crisp basket in, add chicken breasts in single layer inside of Ninja Foodi basket.
5. Close the lid with valve is in the seal position and move the slider to COMBI-STEAM. Select Steam & Crisp set temperature to 180°C/360°F, and time to 10 minutes. Select Start/Stop to begin cooking. (Flip chicken halfway through cooking time)
6. Open lid, top chicken with marinara sauce then cheddar and Parmesan cheese.
7. Close the lid with valve is in the seal position and move the slider to COMBI-STEAM. Select Steam & Crisp set temperature to 180°C/360°F, and time to 5 minutes. Select Start/Stop to begin cooking.
8. Serve with pasta.

PRAWN AND RICE

🕐 **30 Minutes** 👤 **Serves 2**

Ingredients:

- 5 tbsp oil, divided
- 1 large onion, chopped
- 1 large bell pepper, chopped
- 375g uncooked Prawn, peeled and deveined
- 2 tbsp tomato puree
- 2 garlic cloves, minced
- 3 tsp paprika
- ½ tsp red pepper flakes
- 240ml chicken stock
- 250g uncooked rice
- Salt & pepper to taste

Steps:

1. Move the slider to AIR FRY/HOB. Select SEAR/SAUTÉ and set the temperature to HI-5. Select START/STOP to preheat Ninja foodi for 5 minutes, add oil, onion, garlic. Saute for 2 mins. Remove from Ninja Foodi and set aside. Add remaining oil to Ninja. Add Prawn, garlic, and pepper flakes. Cook and stir for 6 minutes. Remove and set aside.
2. Add stock to Ninja. Stir and scrape any stuck pieces. Add rice, tomato puree and paprika. Stir.
3. Close the lid with valve is in the seal position and move the slider to pressure. Cook on high for 8 mins. Select DELAYED RELEASE and set time for 10 mins.Select Start/Stop to begin cooking.
4. Move slider to Air Fry/HOB to unlock the lid, then carefully open it.
5. Open lid, add Prawn and pepper mixture, stir gently, serve.

PRAWN STEW

🕐 **20 Minutes** 👤 **Serves 2**

Ingredients:

- 1 garlic clove, minced
- 1 onion, chopped
- 250g tinned tomatoes, crushed
- 240ml vegetable stock
- ½ tsp turmeric powder
- 450g Prawn, peeled and deveined
- ½ tsp coriander, ground
- ½ tsp dried thyme
- ½ tsp dried basil
- Salt & pepper to taste

Steps:

1. Move the slider to AIR FRY/HOB. Select SEAR/SAUTÉ and set the temperature to HI-5. Select START/STOP to preheat Ninja foodi for 5 minutes, add oil, onion, garlic. Saute for 2 mins. Add all remaining ingredients.
2. Close the lid with valve is in the seal position and move the slider to pressure. Cook on high for 3 mins. Use the arrows to select PRESSURE RELEASE and select QUICK RELEASE.Select Start/Stop to begin cooking.
3. Serve topped with fresh coriander.

FISH PIE

🕐 **50 Minutes** 👤 **Serves 6**

Ingredients:

- 1 kg maris piper potatoes , peeled and chopped
- 250ml water
- 4 tbsp butter
- 4tbsp double cream
- 500ml milk
- 2 salmon fillets, boneless
- 2 haddock fillet, boneless
- 15 prawns, devained

- 40g plain flour
- 180g grated cheddar cheese
- Salt & pepper to taste

Steps:

1. Put the potatoes, water and salt in Ninja Foodi pot.
2. Close the lid with valve is in the seal position and move the slider to pressure. Cook on high for 7 minutes. Use the arrows to select PRESSURE RELEASE and select QUICK RELEASE. Select Start/Stop to begin cooking.
3. Move slider to Air Fry/HOB to unlock the lid, then carefully open it.
4. Drain potatoes and transfer to a bowl, add butter, double cream, salt, pepper to taste. Mash and cover. Wipe out pot and return to Ninja.
5. Move the slider to AIR FRY/HOB. Select SEAR/SAUTÉ and set the temperature to medium high. Select START/STOP to preheat Ninja foodi for 3 minutes, add oil, add flour and sauté for 1 minute. Gradually stir in milk, cook for a few minutes until thickened.
6. Select SEAR/SAUTÉ and set to low-medium, add salmon, haddock, prawns, season with salt & pepper and simmer for 3 minutes. Top with the mashed potatoes, and sprinkle with cheddar cheese.
7. Close the lid and move the slider to AIR FRY/HOB. Select AIR FRY, set the temperature to 190°C/375°F, and set the time to 20 minutes. Press START/STOP to begin cooking.

FISH TAGINE

🕐 25 Minutes 👤 Serves 4

Ingredients:

- 2 tbsp olive oil
- 1 large onion, finely chopped
- 1 (800g) tinned tomatoes, drained and chopped
- 3 garlic cloves, minced
- 3 tsp smoked paprika
- 2 tsp ground cumin
- 1 kg sea bass or halibut, cut into 5-cm chunks
- Handful chopped fresh cilantro
- 2 tbsp chopped fresh parsley
- 1 medium carrot, chopped
- 2 tbsp lemon juice
- 12 green olives, halved & pitted
- Salt & pepper to taste

Steps:

1. Move the slider to AIR FRY/HOB. Select SEAR/SAUTÉ and set the temperature to HI-5. Select START/STOP to preheat Ninja foodi for 5 minutes, add oil, onion, garlic, paprika, cumin, salt, & pepper. Saute for 2 mins. Add all remaining ingredients.

2. Close the lid with valve is in the seal position and move the slider to pressure. Cook on high for 8 mins. Use the arrows to select PRESSURE RELEASE and select QUICK RELEASE.Select Start/Stop to begin cooking.

3. Serve hot with rice.

SEAFOOD STEW

🕐 20 Minutes 👤 Serves 6

Ingredients:

- 1700g cod or striped bass (rinsed and cut into 5 cm chunks)
- 450g prawns (peeled and deveined)
- 15 Little Clams
- 3 tbsp. olive oil
- 1 bay leaf
- 2 tsp. paprika
- 1 medium onion (chopped)
- 1 small green bell pepper (thinly sliced)
- 250g tomatoes (diced)
- 3 garlic cloves (minced)
- 240ml fish stock
- Salt & pepper to taste

Steps:

1. Move the slider to AIR FRY/HOB. Select SEAR/SAUTÉ and set the temperature to HI-5. Select START/STOP to preheat Ninja foodi for 5 minutes, add oil, add pay leaf and paprika and stir. Add onion, bell pepper, tomatoes, and season with salt & pepper. Cook until the onion is softened. Add stock and with a wooden spoon, scrape up pieces stuck to bottom of pot. Put the clams and prawns in pot.

2. Season the fish with salt & pepper, then add it on top of the clams and prawns.

3. Close the lid with valve is in the seal position and move the slider to pressure. Cook on high for 8 mins. Select DELAYED RELEASE and set time for 10 mins.Select Start/Stop to begin cooking.

4. Move slider to Air Fry/HOB to unlock the lid, then carefully open it.

5. Open lid, stir, drizzle with olive oil and sprinkle with coriander leaf before serving.

SAUSAGE AND PRAWN GUMBO

Ingredients:

🕐 30 Minutes 👤 Serves 4

- 1 tbsp olive oil
- 1 bell pepper, chopped
- 1 onion, chopped
- 2 stalks celery, chopped
- 3 cloves garlic, minced
- 375g sausage, sliced
- 1 (425g) tin crushed tomatoes
- 350ml chicken stock
- 2 tsp Cajun seasoning
- 2 bay leaves
- ½ tsp dried oregano
- ½ tsp dried thyme
- ½ tsp dried basil
- 1 tsp hot sauce
- 1 tbsp Worcestershire sauce
- 300g prawn, peeled and deveined
- Salt & pepper to taste

Steps:

1. Move the slider to AIR FRY/HOB. Select SEAR/SAUTÉ and set the temperature to HI-5. Select START/STOP to preheat Ninja foodi for 5 minutes, add oil, onion, celery, garlic and sausage, saute until browned. Add all remaining ingredients (except prawns).
2. Close the lid with valve is in the seal position and move the slider to pressure. Cook on high for 5 mins. Use the arrows to select PRESSURE RELEASE and select QUICK RELEASE.Select Start/Stop to begin cooking. Open lid, add prawn. lose lid, cook on high pressure for 3 mins. Release pressure quickly.
3. Add salt and pepper to taste. Serve hot .

CORNISH CRAB BISQUE

Ingredients:

🕐 40 Minutes 👤 Serves 4

- 2 Tbsp olive oil
- 1 onion, chopped
- 1 fennel bulb, chopped
- 1 carrot, chopped
- 2 bay leaves
- 1 garlic clove, minced
- 3 Tbsp tomato purée
- 200g fresh crabmeat
- 1 pinch of saffron
- 1 liter fish stock
- 100ml double cream
- 1 zest lemon
- 1 tbsp lemon juice
- Salt & pepper to taste

Steps:

1. Move the slider to AIR FRY/HOB. Select SEAR/SAUTÉ and set the temperature to HI-5. Select START/STOP to preheat Ninja foodi for 5 minutes, add oil. Add fennel, onion, and carrots and saute for 5 minutes, add garlic and cook for one minute. Add all remaining ingredients (except double cream), salt, and pepper. Mix until combined.
2. Close the lid with valve is in the seal position and move the slider to pressure. Cook on high for 13 mins. Use the arrows to select PRESSURE RELEASE and select QUICK RELEASE.Select Start/Stop to begin cooking. Move slider to Air Fry/HOB to unlock the lid, then carefully open it.
3. Open the lid, add the double cream. Stir until combined. Blend with blender until smooth.

CULLEN SKINK

 15 Minutes Serves 4

Ingredients:

- 1 onion, (chopped)
- 2 leeks, (chopped)
- 2 potatoes, (peeled & chopped)
- 200g Neeps, (chopped)
- 1 tbsp oil
- 375g Haddock
- 600ml fish stock
- 200ml whole milk
- 2 tsp thyme
- 1 tbsp parsley, (chopped)
- Salt & pepper to taste

Steps:

1. Move the slider to AIR FRY/HOB. Select SEAR/SAUTÉ and set the temperature to HI-5. Select START/STOP to preheat Ninja foodi for 5 minutes, add oil, onion, leek, potatoes, neeps and sauté for 2-3 minutes. Add Haddock, fish stock, thyme and salt & black pepper and stir.

2. Close the lid with valve is in the seal position and move the slider to pressure. Cook on high for 8 minutes. Use the arrows to select PRESSURE RELEASE and select QUICK RELEASE.Select Start/Stop to begin cooking.

3. Move slider to Air Fry/HOB to unlock the lid, then carefully open it.

4. Open the lid, Remove the Haddock, add the milk. Stir until combined. Blend with blender until smooth.

5. Transfer into bowls then serve topped with Haddock and parsley.

BERMUDA FISH CHOWDER

 15 Minutes Serves 6

Ingredients:

- 500ml fish stock
- 1 (450g) tin crushed tomatoes
- 80ml ketchup
- 3 potatoes, peeled & cubed
- 1 onion, chopped
- 2 celery, chopped
- 2 large carrots, chopped
- 2 green bell pepper, chopped
- 2 ½ tsp Worcestershire sauce
- 2 bay leaves
- ½ tsp dried thyme
- 1 tsp curry powder
- 500g lean fish fillets, chopped
- Salt & pepper to taste

Steps:

1. In your Ninja Foodi, add all ingredients. (except fish)

2. Close the lid with valve is in the seal position and move slider to pressure. Cook on high for 5 minutes.

3. Use the arrows to select PRESSURE RELEASE and select QUICK RELEASE.Select Start/Stop to begin cooking. Move slider to Air Fry/HOB to unlock the lid, then carefully open it.

4. Open the lid. Add fish. close lid and cook on high pressure for another 3 mins, quickly release pressure.

5. Open the lid, stir.Transfer into bowls then serve.

FISH & CHIPS

🕐 18 Minutes   👤 Serves 6

Ingredients:

- 900g cod fillets
- 60g flour
- 30g cornsflour
- 1 tbsp sugar
- 120ml cold water
- 1 egg
- 100g plain flour
- 100g breadcrumbs
- Salt & pepper to taste

For the chips

- 1¼ kg, peeled and cut into ½ inch/1.5cm long fries
- Salt & pepper to taste

Steps:

1. Soak potatoes in a bowl of cold water for 30 minutes.
2. In a bowl, whisk 60g flour and cornflour. In another bowl, stir together 100g flour, garlic powder, onion powder, salt, pepper, and Bicarbonate of soda. Pour in cold water and stir to combine. (if too thick add more water)
3. Dredge each fish piece in flour mixture, then in the batter. Place the fish pieces back in the flour mixture to fully coat.
4. Line ninja Cook & Crisp basket with parchment paper and spray with cooking spray. add fish into basket. Spray tops of fish with cooking spray. Add basket in Ninja Foodi.
5. Close the lid and move the slider to AIR FRY/HOB. Select AIR FRY, set the temperature to 190°C/375°F, and set the time to 10 minutes. Press START/STOP to begin cooking.
6. Remove from ninja, transfer to a plate and cover with foil. Set aside.
7. Close the lid and move the slider to AIR FRY/HOB. Select AIR FRY, set the temperature to 190°C/375°F, and set the time to 14 minutes until golden brown and crispy. Press START/STOP to begin cooking. Flipping halfway through cooking time.
8. Serve the fish and chips.

CAULIFLOWER CHEESE

🕐 30 Minutes   👤 Serves 6

Ingredients:

- 1 head cauliflower, cut into small florets
- 230g grated cheddar/gouda cheese
- 120g cream cheese, softened
- 3 tbsp butter
- 60ml double cream
- Salt & pepper to taste

Steps:

1. Add 500ml water to Ninja Foodi pot. Add Foodi Cook & Crisp basket in, add cauliflour florets in basket.

2. Close lid and cook on high pressure for 1 minute. Use the arrows to select PRESSURE RELEASE and select QUICK RELEASE. Select Start/Stop to begin cooking. Move slider to Air Fry/HOB to unlock the lid, then carefully open it.

3. In a saucepan over high heat, add flour, mustard powder and milk. Stir & bring to boil, reduce heat and simmer, continuously stirring for 2 mins until thickens.

4. Take Cook & Crisp basket out. Drain water out of Foodi pot. Add cauliflower into the Foodi pot and top with cheese sauce. Add more grated cheese on top.

5. Close the lid with valve is in the seal position and move the slider to COMBI-STEAM. Select Steam & Crisp set temperature to 190°C/375°F, and time to 13 minutes. Select Start/Stop to begin cooking. Once finished, Serve.

MUSHY PEAS

🕐 40 Minutes   👤 Serves 4

Ingredients:

- 300 g Dried Marrowfat peas, soaked overnight with (or without) the soaking tablets.
- 600ml water
- ½ tsp Malt vinegar or Apple cider vinegar
- Salt & pepper to taste

Steps:

1. Rinse the soaked peas in cold water.

2. In your slow cooker, add peas and water. stir.

3. Close lid and cook on high pressure for 15 minute. Let pressure release naturally. Select Start/Stop to begin cooking. Move slider to Air Fry/HOB to unlock the lid, then carefully open it.

4. Open lid, and season as desired with salt, pepper and vinegar and serve straight away.

AUBERGINE & CHICKPEA STEW

🕐 30 Minutes 👤 Serves 4

Ingredients:

- 375g canned chickpeas, drained
- 2 tbsp oil
- 2 onions, chopped
- 6 garlic cloves, minced
- 1 tsp ground cinnamon
- 1 parsley bunch, stalks finely chopped
- 2 tsp smoked paprika
- 2 tsp smoked paprika
- 3 medium aubergines, chopped into 4cm pieces
- 2 (375g) tins chopped tomatoes
- 1 lemon juice
- Salt & pepper to taste

Steps:

1. Move the slider to AIR FRY/HOB. Select SEAR/SAUTÉ and set the temperature to HI-5. Select START/STOP to preheat Ninja foodi for 5 minutes, add oil cook onions until soft. Add garlic, spices and cook for 1 min.

2. Add all remaining ingredients. Mix until combined.

3. Close lid and cook on high pressure for 5 minute. Let pressure release naturally. Select Start/Stop to begin cooking. Move slider to Air Fry/HOB to unlock the lid, then carefully open it.

4. Garnish with chopped parsley and serve with rice.

PUMPKIN SOUP

🕐 15 Minutes 👤 Serves 6

Ingredients:

- 1 onion, chopped
- 2 garlic clove, minced,
- 2 carrots, chopped
- 1 ¼ kg pumpkin, cubed
- 1 tsp cumin, ground
- 1 tsp paprika
- 700ml chicken stock
- 240ml double cream

Steps:

1. In Ninja Foodi, add all ingredients except double cream. Mix until combined.

2. Close the lid with valve is in the seal position and move the slider to pressure. Cook on high for 6 minutes. Use the arrows to select PRESSURE RELEASE and select QUICK RELEASE.Select Start/Stop to begin cooking.

3. Move slider to Air Fry/HOB to unlock the lid, then carefully open it.

4. Let cool slightly, the puree with hand/regular blender. Add more stock until desired consistency is reached. Add double cream and stir.

TOMATO BASIL SOUP

🕐 **30 Minutes** 👤 **Serves 5**

Ingredients:

- 2 medium onions, finely diced
- 1 tsp red pepper flakes
- 3 tbsp olive oil
- 3 large carrots, peeled & finely diced
- Salt & pepper to taste
- 4 whole peeled cloves garlic
- 15 basil leaves
- 3 (800g) tins whole peeled tomatoes
- 1 liter chicken stock
- 120ml double cream

Steps:

1. Move the slider to AIR FRY/HOB. Select SEAR/SAUTÉ and set the temperature to HI-5. Select START/STOP to preheat Ninja foodi for 5 minutes, add oil, saute onion and carrots for 5 mins. Add garlic and cook for 1 min. Add all remaining ingredients. (except double cream)

2. Close the lid with valve is in the seal position and move the slider to pressure. Cook on high for 15 minutes. Select DELAYED RELEASE and set time for 10 mins. Select Start/Stop to begin cooking.

3. Let cool slightly, the puree with hand/regular blender. Add cream. Stir and serve.

CARROT & SWEET POTATO SOUP

🕐 **30 Minutes** 👤 **Serves 4**

Ingredients:

- 1 onion, chopped
- 6 celery sticks, chopped
- 4 carrots, chopped
- 3 sweet potatoes, chopped
- 600ml chicken/vegetable stock
- 2 garlic cloves, minced
- 1 tsp ground ginger
- 1 tsp chilli flakes
- 1 tbsp butter
- 120ml double cream

Steps:

1. Move the slider to AIR FRY/HOB. Select SEAR/SAUTÉ and set the temperature to HI-5. Select START/STOP to preheat Ninja foodi for 5 minutes, add oil, saute onion, celery and carrots for 5 mins. Add garlic, spices and cook for 1 min. Add all remaining ingredients (except double cream)

2. Close the lid with valve is in the seal position and move the slider to pressure. Cook on high for 12 minutes. Let pressure release naturally. Select Start/Stop to begin cooking.

3. Let cool slightly, the puree with hand/regular blender. Add double cream and stir. Serve with a swirl of double cream.

POTATO & LEEK SOUP

⏱ 40 Minutes 👤 Serves 6

Ingredients:

- 3 tbsp butter
- 2 large leeks
- 3 garlic cloves, minced
- 600g potatoes, peeled & chopped
- 2 tsp dried oregano

- 2 tsp dried thyme
- 2 bay leaves
- 1 litre chicken stock,
- 240ml double cream
- 200g cheese, grated
- Salt & pepper to taste

Steps:

1. Move the slider to AIR FRY/HOB. Select SEAR/SAUTÉ and set the temperature to HI-5. Select START/STOP to preheat Ninja foodi for 5 minutes, add oil, saute leeks for 4 mins. Add garlic and cook for 1 min. Add all remaining ingredients (except double cream and cheese)

2. Close the lid with valve is in the seal position and move the slider to pressure. Cook on high for 7 minutes. Select DELAYED RELEASE and set time for 10 mins. Select Start/Stop to begin cooking.

3. Open lid, then puree with hand/regular blender. Add more stock until desired consistency is reached.

4. Add the cream and cheese to the soup and stir. Serve.

CAULIFLOWER & BROCCOLI SOUP

⏱ 35 Minutes 👤 Serves 6

Ingredients:

- 1 head cauliflower, cut into large florets
- 1 head broccoli, cut into large florets
- 6 garlic cloves

- 1 onion, diced
- 750ml chicken stock
- 225g cream cheese
- 100g grated cheese

Steps:

1. In your Ninja Foodi, add all ingredients except cheeses. Mix until combined.

2. Close the lid with valve is in the seal position and move the slider to pressure. Cook on high for 5 minutes. Select DELAYED RELEASE and set time for 15 mins. Select Start/Stop to begin cooking.

3. Open lid, add cheeses, then puree with hand/regular blender. Add more stock until desired consistency is reached.

BUTTERNUT SQUASH SOUP

 20 Minutes 👤 Serves 5

Ingredients:

- 1 kg butternut squash peeled and small cubed
- 1 onion, chopped
- 500ml chicken stock
- 1 Tbsp brown sugar
- 500ml half cream
- Salt & pepper to taste

Steps:

1. In your Ninja Foodi, add all ingredients except half cream. Mix until combined.
2. Close the lid with valve is in the seal position and move the slider to pressure. Cook on high for 8 minutes. Use the arrows to select PRESSURE RELEASE and select QUICK RELEASE.Select Start/Stop to begin cooking.
3. Open lid, then puree with hand/regular blender.
4. Add the cream to the soup and stir. Serve.

CAULIFLOWER CHEESE SOUP

🕐 30 Minutes 👤 Serves 6

Ingredients:

- 1 liter chicken stock
- 1 head cauliflower cut into chunks
- 3 leeks, chopped

- 2 garlic cloves, minced
- 2 shredded sharp cheddar cheese
- 120ml double cream
- Salt & pepper to taste

Steps:

1. Move the slider to AIR FRY/HOB. Select SEAR/SAUTÉ and set the temperature to HI-5. Select START/STOP to preheat Ninja foodi for 5 minutes, add oil, saute onion until soft. Add garlic and cook for 1 min. Add all remaining ingredients (except double cream and cheese)
2. Close the lid with valve is in the seal position and move the slider to pressure. Cook on high for 5 minutes. Select DELAYED RELEASE and set time for 10 mins. Select Start/Stop to begin cooking.
3. Open lid, then puree with hand/regular blender. Add more stock until desired consistency is reached.
4. Add double cream and cheese. Stir and serve.

CARROT GINGER SOUP

 Ingredients: 🕐 35 Minutes 👤 Serves 4

- 1 kg carrots, chopped
- 2 onions, chopped
- 2 garlic clove, minced
- 50g fresh ginger, peeled & sliced
- 1 liter chicken stock
- 250ml double cream
- Salt & pepper to taste

Steps:

1. In your Ninja Foodi, add all ingredients except cream. Mix until combined.
2. Close the lid with valve is in the seal position and move the slider to pressure. Cook on high for 10 minutes. Let pressure release naturally. Select Start/Stop to begin cooking.
3. Open lid, then puree with hand/regular blender. Add more stock if its too thick.
4. Add the cream to the soup and stir. Season with more salt & pepper if desired. Serve.

PARSNIP STILTON SOUP

Ingredients: 🕐 25 Minutes 👤 Serves 4

- 1 onion, diced
- 4 parsnips, peeled and cubed
- 2 potatoes, peeled and cubed
- 1 bay leaf
- 1 liter chicken stock
- 250ml double cream

- 125g Stilton cheese, crumbled
- Salt & pepper to taste

Steps:

1. Move the slider to AIR FRY/HOB. Select SEAR/SAUTÉ and set the temperature to HI-5. Select START/STOP to preheat Ninja foodi for 5 minutes, add oil, saute onion until soft. Add all remaining ingredients (except double cream and cheese)
2. Close the lid with valve is in the seal position and move the slider to pressure. Cook on high for 12 minutes. Select DELAYED RELEASE and set time for 10 mins. Select Start/Stop to begin cooking.
3. Open lid, remove bay leaf then puree with hand/regular blender. Add more stock until desired consistency is reached. Add double cream and Stilton. Stir and serve.

Printed in Great Britain
by Amazon

12954069R00052